LIVING WITH ZEST
IN AN
EMPTY NEST

LIVING WITH ZEST IN AN EMPTY NEST

by Jean Kinney

HAWTHORN BOOKS, INC.
Publishers
NEW YORK

Dedicated with a salute
to the millions of parents
whose children are on their own
and who are finding with delight that
life is far from over
in an empty nest

NINE THINGS THIS BOOK WILL HELP YOU TO DO

1. Shed apprehension about the future the way a snake sheds its old skin.

2. Delight old and new friends with a home that's a "conversation piece."

3. Get more enjoyment out of every day as your individual life-style becomes more pronounced.

4. Move from the back seat to the front seat in the eyes of your family.

5. Make three new friends each month in a fascinating new interest-matching "game."

6. Take twelve luxury trips this year for little more per trip than a day at the ball park.

7. Bank more money next year than ever before, even though prices spiral.

8. Enjoy *Good Living* in all its aspects as a matter of course.

9. Find looking ahead a pleasure every single night.

CONTENTS

PART FIVE: An Ever-Widening Circle of
People You Like to Be With

PART SIX: Looking at the World with a
"Seeing Eye" Wherever You
Happen to Be

PART SEVEN: No Final Retirement Plan
Ever!

INTRODUCTION:

WHAT IS THIS BOOK ABOUT?

This is a book for mothers whose children are nearing or have ended their years of dependence. For these women, freedom from the need for full-time homemaking can mean either adventure or apathy. Which will it be for you? As you read, look into the future.

Hundreds of specific suggestions for enriching your life are contained in these pages. Many are worry-erasers; some are for serious projects; a few are downright frivolous. All can help you to rekindle the impulse toward delight you were born with. You will be enthusiastic about living.

You're joining a club

If the last of your children is about to leave home, you will soon be joining a vast club. In America, alone, there are more than thirty million women living in empty nests all of whom have three things in common. They are over forty; they have reached one major goal in the raising of their children; as newcomers to empty nests, they can look forward to more years coming up than girls born in Revolutionary days could count on for an entire lifetime.

With all of this new time to do anything they want to do, women by all odds should be welcoming these bonus years with a glad cry. Their mothers didn't get this second chance, nor did their grandmothers or any women ever before. Yet, talk to the next five women you meet whose children are growing and going, and you will be fortunate to find one who is enthusiastic about reaching out for a new adventure. The other four will be totally unaware that opportunity knocks; and even as they listen to your good tidings, many will be apathetic and some will even be depressed. In view of the truth, why should this be?

Explanation from psychologists

The very thought of a home's being emptied of children fills many mothers with a feeling of loneliness, psychologists say. It drains them of enthusiasm for anything new. Like the sixty-five-year-old man who feels uprooted when it comes time for him to walk away from his lifetime work, the forty-five-year-old woman feels disoriented as her mothering days come to a close. Unless she has a definite plan for what she wants to do next, the syndrome* triggered by the loss of her children and her "mothering" job and by the reminder of advancing age that comes with grandmotherhood is bound to get to her. Luckily, there is a remedy.

The power of positive action

"The same thoughts come to most middle-aged women," says Dr. Josephine Ross, psychologist at Connecticut's Housatonic Psychiatric Center at Lakeville. "It's what they do about them that makes the difference."

* Referred to by sociologists as "the empty nest syndrome."

One mother weeps when her children won't come over on Sunday for dinner; another takes a trip. One woman sits all day in front of a television set; another goes back to school. One wife reads the life expectancy table for men and worries about widowhood; another rejoices that her husband can look forward to a longer life than his father before him, and she makes plans for a new house. In each case, depression goes when action is taken.

Sit still with your thoughts of bygone years, and you will sit alone. Welcome these new years as a time when anything is possible and you will open the door to adventure. To provide you with the key to this door, never available to women before, is the purpose of this book.

More than a book, it's a plan

This is not a book written, like most books, to inform or entertain. It is an action book, a revolutionary life-enriching plan that tells what steps to take to effect an unprecedented change in your mental attitude and, thus, in your life. Follow the simple rules spelled out, and your feeling of self-worth will grow. So will your sure knowledge that anything is possible.

Sure-footed steps to a happier life

The book is separated into seven parts, each one of which deals with a different area of your life directly related to your overall happiness. Take one step after another as recommended and you will unconsciously begin to absorb and apply the sound principles that underscore each prescribed life-expanding rule. By the time you finish Part Seven, you will be aware of an unprecedented change in every department of your life.

1. You (and your husband) will just plain feel better.

2. Your home will be an out-and-out joy.
3. Money will be no problem.
4. You will be conscious of a talent you were never aware of before.
5. Your friends and family will find new things about you to love and respect.
6. You will get far more joy out of traveling.
7. Retirement (wherever you want to live) will pose no problem.

Make notes as you read

Keep a small notebook or pad of paper beside you as you read. On every page you will find suggestions for empty nesters that are bound to make sense.

All recommendations are simple and easy to remember, and there is no reason to copy each one, but in each of the seven parts there will be at least one recommendation that penetrates your consciousness like a beacon of light. Write down the recommendation that hits you. Eventually, your notebook will contain at least seven specific rules that will add up to a recipe that is custom-made for your particular life-style.

Building your life from the inside out

Let's say that for the past twenty-five years you have been rearing a family and feel no guilt now about doing something on your own, but you don't know exactly how and where to begin. Dead set against doing something "just to fill up time," you want specific suggestions about what to do next that will fit neatly into a way of life exactly right for you. Obviously, you have a strong sense of independence, with a life-force that flows from the inside out. Whether your need is for more education, an economic lift, or a wider circle of acquaintances, you will find the way as you read.

You are fortunate if you are a self-sufficient woman with an adventurous mind. Undoubtedly, you have not looked for fulfillment only through the accomplishments of your children in the past and you will not do so in the future. All you need are a few concrete suggestions, and you can live life to the fullest.

This is not to say that the mother who has lived vicariously is lost. She may feel bereft in her empty nest, and she may have to do some deep probing to find out who she is and what she really wants, but she can find her answer. The method is here.

As an empty nester, I know from doing some pretty deep digging myself that the more a woman concentrates on her own aptitudes and wants, the less likely she is to be bored. Therefore, I will encourage no reader to copy the life-style of another. It simply doesn't work.

Compare the way you do things with the approach of others, and you will see that even though your house or apartment may be similar in size and shape to ten others close by, your way of life is unique. To paraphrase the seventeenth-century essayist François Fénelon: "Your style is as much a part of you as the throbbing of your pulse." This deeply entrenched you is going to remain the same no matter what your external conditions, and this book respects this fact. Actually, it encourages every reader, wherever or however she may live, to build out from what she is to a fuller life than she has ever known.

The real meaning of zest

Empty nesters who function with vitality and enthusiasm live with a *sense of abundance*. They may not have the most money, but they never live with lack. They may not be the most robust, but their talk is never sick. They may not have a crowd around, but their friends are always there. Naturally, such people savor every day, and enthusiasm comes easy. This is the meaning of zest.

You will begin to function at your optimum as you come to understand various elements in your life that affect your overall sense of well-being. Then, as you synchronize and refashion these elements, your life-style will begin to reflect the real you, and the opportunity will come to do what deep down you have always wanted to do. Once this happens, you will never be bored again, and *you will live with zest for the rest of your days.*

When a goal is reached in life,
you may come to a temporary standstill,
but you cannot remain at rest
while you still live. For to live
is to function. That is all there is to living.

Gist of radio address
given by Oliver Wendell Holmes, Jr.,
on his ninetieth birthday
(March 8, 1931)

PART ONE

GOOD HEALTH: THE GREATEST ASSET OF ALL

1

WHEN YOU'RE PHYSICALLY FIT, YOU CAN COPE WITH ANYTHING

Your health is the retaining wall that keeps your world from crumbling. When your vitality is at its peak, you are eager for the day to start when you wake up in the morning, and you aren't shaken by much of anything as the hours go by. But if you feel physically uncomfortable for any reason, real or imagined, you will be vaguely anxious most of the time. So guard your health above all else. Physical fitness is your most important asset by far!

Like your age, a chronic disability such as arthritis, a bad heart, or limited hearing or vision is something you can't do much about. So for your purpose here, define good health as it applies to you personally. Are you functioning each day at your optimum within your personal, physical, and mental framework? If so, your life holds unlimited promise. If not, it's time for a change.

One advantage: You know what to expect

After you have lived with yourself for four or five or more decades, few new allergies turn up to surprise you, few headaches lay you low that you can't explain, few stomach upsets come that you can't trace back. You, better than anyone else, are aware of your strengths and your weaknesses. Long years of familiarity help you to know how much strenuous exercise you can stand, how much sleep you need, what foods do or don't agree with you. With this stored-up knowledge, there is no better diagnostician, dietitian, or nurse for you than you. So it follows that with your objective care, you should be in the pink of condition.

Do you fall short? If so, you are either paying too little attention to familiar warning signs or you are living with a negative condition you do not understand. To help you with your self-diagnosis, answer these twelve questions:

Questions about your health

1. Are you free of any illness, disability, or deformity that gives you more difficulty than it gives the average person of your age? (If not, can your present condition be corrected?)
2. Do you come from a long-lived family?
3. Is your daily environment (including climate, available food and medication, good sleeping conditions, lack of physical and mental stress) about as satisfactory as you can imagine it to be? (If not, can you do something to change present conditions?)
4. Are you a good eater?
5. Are you a good sleeper?

6. Are you no more than ten pounds overweight or underweight?
7. Do you get plenty of exercise?
8. Is it easy for you to avoid overeating, overdrinking, oversmoking, overworking?
9. Do you have less than the average number of colds and other temporary setbacks?
10. Do you snap back in a hurry from a temporary illness?
11. Is worry something you simply don't do?
12. Do you have at least five *active* interests that you thoroughly enjoy? (Examples: a job, gardening, regular bridge sessions, painting or some other creative work, a volunteer project, church work, etc.)

Count your yes answers

If you have more than nine yes answers, your health is about as good as you can wish for, and the prognosis for your continuing well-being is excellent. If you have fewer than nine yes answers, don't despair. With the exception of questions numbers 1 and 2, all no answers can be switched to yes as you absorb the book's principles.

Keeping yourself in good condition is a form of unselfishness

The woman who baby-sits for her grandchildren whenever she is asked, waits on her husband hand and foot, and nurses every friend who knocks at her door is no heroine. Eventually, she collapses, and when that happens she becomes a problem to others. So, in the long run, neglecting self to give all to those around you is no mark of nobility. Quite the contrary—letting yourself get run-down through overwork or neglect leads to dependency. Martyrdom in any woman eventually works a hardship on her friends, her children, her husband, everyone. So, to be truly unselfish, take care of yourself. Naturally, you won't forget the needs of others, but whenever possible, you will make it easy for them to take care of themselves as you take care of yourself.

What to do about minor disorders
that affect you and others your age

The nine aches and upsets that are most apt to cause discomfort to you, your husband, or a visiting friend in your age bracket are: (1) headache, (2) sore throat, (3) an aching back, (4) muscular discomfort, (5) upset stomach, (6) dizziness, (7) constipation, (8) a cold, (9) a cut or burn. The following remedies can prevent such upsets from becoming a real problem. These suggested relief givers are recommended by doctors and pharmacists and, in most cases, are available at your drugstore without a prescription. (If you know from past experience that a suggested drug does not agree with you, avoid it.)

COMFORT ROBBERS	RELIEF GIVERS
1. Tension headache	Take aspirin or similar pain killer, strong coffee or caffeine tablet, and Tums or other antacid. (Caffeine helps hypertensive headache and is prescribed by neurosurgeons for postoperative headaches. Antacid relieves stomach jarred by both aspirin and caffeine.)
2. Sore throat	Gargle with salt water. Take antihistamine tablet or use nose drops to stop postnasal drip that leads to throat discomfort. For severe sore throat (usually associated with high fever and overall systematic symptoms) call doctor, who

COMFORT ROBBERS   RELIEF GIVERS

will probably prescribe penicillin, which is not a one-shot dose but must be taken for several consecutive days.

3. Aching back

Take aspirin or similar analgesic to decrease pain. Take hot shower or apply heating pad; sleep on firm mattress or bed board.

4. Muscular discomfort

When tension tightens head, chest, or neck muscles, take sedative and have professional or home massage. (When massaging at home, stroke with electric vibrator, if possible, in direction of heart, not toward extremities.)

5. Upset stomach

If possible, induce vomiting. Then substitute tea and toast or clear hot soup for a couple of meals. Take Maalox (which is a combination of milk of magnesia and aluminum hydroxide) or other nonlaxative antacid. (Should you have abdominal pain for several hours, do not take a laxative, call physician.)

6. Dizziness

This is a tricky one. Can be caused by sinus infection, inner ear disturbance, arthritic condition in back of neck, high blood pressure, or vision difficulty. If acute, lie down immediately and wait for doctor. (If problem is arthritis, he may prescribe collar.)

7. Constipation

For immediate relief, use glycerine suppository. For long-term help, eat natural laxative foods like yogurt, molasses, honey, bulk cereals (bran), prunes, and lots of fresh fruit.

8. A cold

The old remedy of aspirin, bed rest, and lots of fruit juice is still best. As an annual preventative, take cold and/or flu shots.

9. A burn or cut

For minor burns, use any good pharmaceutical remedy or your grandmother's recipe, cold, strong tea. (Tannic acid washes away dead skin which attracts germs.) For small cut, apply Band-Aid. Stop bleeding with styptic pencil or hair spray. (Hair spray freezes wound, leaves glaze.) For a serious cut, elevate extremity above heart to help stop bleeding and apply pressure to wound.

For any serious problem, call your doctor immediately. But for a simple upset, administer any of the above remedies with security. According to Dr. Jack Finkelstein, assistant professor at Flower and Fifth Avenue Hospitals, New York City, complaints to anticipate when traveling (or when friends are visiting you) are sore throat and upset stomach. Keep a kit of simple remedies in your travel bag and at home for guests.

Don't fuss

Keep simple pain relievers in your medicine chest just as you keep staples in your kitchen cupboard, but once these remedies are stashed away, forget about them except in emergency. And don't constantly fuss over yourself, your husband, or your friends. Do what's called for as needed, but don't talk about the catastrophes of others nor about every little ache and pain of your own, which is more of a sign of advancing age than the aches and pains themselves.

Take a commonsense attitude toward health maintenance. This includes keeping your doctor's telephone number beside your telephone, the numbers of your insurance policies on a card in your billfold next to a record of any physical disability like diabetes which you may have, and your health and hospital insurance policies in your desk (not in your safe-deposit box). Once you tick off these simple precautions, get on with the business of living.

Five nearby health protectors
no empty nester should be without

Five names and numbers which should be close to your telephone wherever you live are those of your family doctor, a dentist you have confidence in, an optometrist who knows your eyeglass prescription, an osteopath, chiropractor, or masseuse, and a good foot doctor. In a new community, finding an excellent person in each of these categories may take some doing, even some traveling to nearby towns, but the security you feel when you have confidence that an expert will be available when needed makes the search worthwhile.

A general practitioner who knows you inside and out will administer cold and flu shots as needed, can prescribe drugs by telephone to your local pharmacist, and will keep your medical history on hand for the convenience of another doctor who may be called in his absence. A dentist and optometrist are equally essential. A good masseuse or masseur, chiropractor, or osteopath can provide quick and soothing relief from muscular tension during periods of strain and hard work. A good chiropodist or podiatrist can do as much for your comfort as a masseuse. A simple corn is about as disturbing an ill as flesh is heir to, and the minute your pain tolerance is reached you are going to need help.

A lift for you is a lift for others

Keep physically fit and you will walk taller, breathe deeper, and move along with your arms swinging loose and easy and your head lifted high. Just to look at you will give casual passersby a lift, and you will be a positive joy to those who come in contact with you every day. And now you really have something to contribute, especially to a husband.

"A man may lose confidence in his manhood," says Gaylord Hauser, beauty and health consultant, "when his wife does not seem to invite his attentions, or when she does not bother to make herself attractive, even seductive, just for him." No woman can feel attractive, and certainly she can't feel seductive, when her health is under par. Take simple health precautions, and you will automatically be a better wife.

A man's best wealth

"A good wife," goes an old proverb, "and good health are a man's best wealth." All the way through this book you will find marriage-enriching suggestions, but certainly good health is primary in this closest relationship of all. The odds are high that with good health you will be a good wife. And as a good wife you can help to provide the next requisite for his happiness—*good health for your husband*.

Today's life expectancy statistics for the American male are disturbing. Only a woman who is in good physical shape can provide the emotional and physical environment that experts believe is necessary for the long and happy life of the man she married.

2

A SIMPLE WAY TO BEAT
SOME GRIM STATISTICS

If you are like most wives, you feel closer to your husband in an empty nest than you have for years, and his welfare is uppermost in your mind. Suddenly, one day you look across the table and realize that he is getting older, and statistics that have meant little to you loom large. Is it true that he has fewer years to go than you? Are you destined to spend long years as a widow? How can you beat the odds?

Fact: According to new life-expectancy tables, today's male has seven years less to go than a female. Add to this fact the probability of your husband's being two or three or more years older than you, and thoughts of your being a widow for close to a decade begin to keep you awake nights.

What you want: A life plan that will add years to your husband's life. Is there such a recipe? Not specifically, but there's certainly a clue in any life-expectancy table.

On the day of your husband's birth, assuming he is a new empty nester, a prophet could have promised him a lifetime of about fifty-three years, no longer. But now that he is a fifty-year-old grandfather, he has far more than just three more years to go. Having beaten the rap so far, he has more than twenty-three years ahead of him, the tables say. Furthermore, should he live to be sixty, he will have the promise of not thirteen but more than sixteen years coming up. And so it goes. Each year that your husband lives, he beats the odds against having just a little time left. Finally, when he and you reach eighty-five, your anticipated life expectancy will be about the same, a little more than four years for both.

Obviously, then, if you can help your husband to end each year in better shape than he was at the beginning of that year, you can beat the long-term widowhood rap. The simple way to outwit the grim statistics is to help your husband to outlive them. With this in mind, what can you do?

Four widow-makers to guard against

According to Dr. Ancel Keys, world-known director of physiological hygiene, School of Public Health, University of Minnesota, the four major widow-makers in the United States today are heart disease, lung and bronchial disorders caused by cigarette smoking, firearms, and automobile accidents. By far the most villainous is heart disease, which accounts for 40 percent of all male deaths and makes for the imbalance between women and men over sixty in this country.*

"Between the ages of forty-five and fifty-four," Dr. Keys reports, "the death rate of men is almost double that of women, and between the ages of fifty-five and sixty-four, it *is* double." It is his conviction that the high incidence of coronary heart disease among American men can be cut down with a change in eating and living habits.

---

* There are more than three million more women than men over sixty.

Is your husband headed for a heart attack?

If your husband drives far to his office or commutes, he probably gets up earlier than you and gets his own breakfast (orange juice that you have ready in the refrigerator, coffee, toast, and maybe cereal, egg, or a glass of milk). Because he has reached the peak of his career by now, much of his work is probably desk work, and subordinates come to him, not vice versa. So, after he reaches his office, he moves around little, if at all, until noon when he eats a pleasant lunch preceded perhaps by a drink or two.* Afterward, back he goes to his sit-down job until time to drive or take the train home. By now, you have an excellent dinner waiting. His favorite, maybe steak, baked potato with sour cream, buttered peas, salad with roquefort dressing, and pie—"just this once"—with coffee. After he reads the paper, he goes to bed for a good night's sleep so he can get an early start for the kind of day he loves.

The good life? No, because if your husband is overweight, with blood pressure already on the high side and with too much cholesterol building up in his blood, his chances of having a heart attack in the next ten years are one in two. And if, along with this, he smokes heavily, he's headed for the oxygen tent for sure *unless you help him to do a quick about-face.* Beginning tomorrow, encourage him to work more exercise into his daily regime and cut back on cigarettes, calories, and high cholesterol foods.

---

* There is no special harm in a premeal cocktail, say most doctors, except that it adds calories and makes for the unthought-about eating of a roll and butter, crackers and cheese, or other fat-makers.

The cholesterol theory

Heart specialists have long known that almost all heart attacks can be traced to deposits of cholesterol in the coronary arteries that provide blood for the heart muscles. The situation in the arteries of the brain is similar; eventually, clogged brain arteries result in a stroke. In unusual cases, an inherited flaw accounts for extra amounts of cholesterol in the blood, but in all cases the blood cholesterol level is raised from eating too many saturated fats (butter, eggs, beef, lamb, ice cream, etc.). Believing, anyway, that 30 percent of our daily intake of calories should come from fats, experts recommend unsaturated fats (vegetable oils—except coconut or palm oils—chicken, the "soft" margarines, fish, etc.) rather than saturated fats in a ratio of 2 to 1.

By now, you and your husband have acquired a taste for foods with a high cholesterol level. Harvard nutritionist Dr. Robert B. McGandy, who is a firm believer that proper diet can alter the incidence of coronary heart disease, says that even our baby diets in America contain too much salt and saturated fats. "And every year after that the average American's taste for cholesterol-producing foods becomes more firmly established. Finally, in the dangerous middle-aged years, it takes a terrific effort to switch." Still, to keep that husband around, *the attempt must be made!*

One recent study found that men under fifty with a blood-cholesterol level of over 260 have a six times greater heart attack risk than men of the same age with a reading of 220 or less.* Not only your husband but you will benefit

---

* Finding announced by Dr. William B. Kannel, director of a heart research team that has computed data over a twenty-year period about the heart conditions and living habits of 5,127 men and women in Framingham, Mass.

from a new attention to your eating habits. Women are by no means immune to heart attacks. The odds are the same for them but the risk becomes comparable to that of men twenty years later in life.*

On a low-cholesterol diet, you and your husband will probably experience a weight loss, even though your prime purpose now is to cut down on saturated fats, not calories. Later, you will be given an easy new way to diet, but for now pay particular attention to the fat content, because today we can no more deny that cholesterol deposits in our blood vessels are a heart disease threat than we can discount the evidence that cigarettes are harmful.

Does your husband smoke too much?

More than ten years ago, E. Cuyler Hammond, Vice President, Department of Epidemiology and Biostatistics, for the American Cancer Society, announced findings that proved that the death rate among men from coronary artery disease was 70 percent higher among cigarette smokers than non-smokers and that the lung cancer rate was more than ten times higher. Other reported causes of death which showed an association with cigarette smoking were gastric and duodenal ulcers, certain diseases of the arteries, chronic bronchitis, pulmonary diseases, including pneumonia, emphysema, and influenza, cancer of the bladder, and cirrhosis of the liver. New Studies continue to produce similar findings, and among the volunteers in one project that lasted several years men aged forty-five to fifty-four who smoked a pack or more of cigarettes a day tripled their risk of a lethal coronary attack. The American Cancer Society says now that of our sixty thousand deaths a year from lung cancer,

* Probably due to a sex hormone difference.

75 percent are due to cigarette smoking, and that the rate of death from all pulmonary causes would be even higher if smokers were not dying of other diseases before lung disorders have had a chance to show up. All along the way, the overall death rate of cigarette smokers is 60 percent higher than the death rate of nonsmokers.

According to today's medical researchers, nicotine triggers the release of catecholamine chemicals that cause the heart to stumble and/or stop. Or as one doctor put it: Nicotine constricts the arteries impeding the flow of blood to the heart. Result: Heart tissue is damaged.

So you can bet that if your husband smokes more than five cigarettes a day, he has a higher death risk than a nonsmoker. And if he is under sixty-five and a heavy two-packs-a-day smoker, he may not reach retirement age.

This is depressing only if he will not cut down or stop smoking now. As the Surgeon General's report pointed out a few years ago, "The death risk is diminished by discontinuing smoking." The great majority of doctors agree.

So how do you get your husband to quit?

Nagging will get you no place. Neither will the force-feeding of scare statistics. Still, there are ways to encourage your husband to break the cigarette habit.

1. *Know the facts, so that you can answer alibis with truth.*
    Alibis: (1) I smoke a filter. (2) I smoke a menthol cigarette. (3) I don't inhale. (4) A lot of people get lung cancer who have never smoked. (5) Smog is worse than cigarettes. (6) If it's bad for me, why does my doctor smoke? (7) I'll gain weight. (8) I'll be so tense I'll get an ulcer.

Answers: (1) Filters do not prevent cancer, and
some filter cigarettes contain more tar and nicotine than some nonfilters. (2) Menthol is simply a flavor additive. (3) Most smokers inhale,
even if they don't know it. (The death rate of
persons who say they do not inhale is higher
than that of nonsmokers.) (4) The lung cancer
death rate of nonsmokers is only one-tenth that
of smokers. (5) Even where air pollution is a
problem, 75 percent of the deaths from lung
cancer could be prevented if people had never
smoked cigarettes. (6) It is estimated from
a number of studies that 100,000 doctors have
stopped smoking, more than half of those who
ever smoked. (7) A wife can help by serving
fewer high-calorie meals. (8) More than twice
as many smokers die from peptic ulcers than
nonsmokers.

2. *Don't make it easy for him to smoke.*
Don't keep cigarettes near your husband's favorite
reading place.

3. *Give him a pipe for his birthday or Christmas.*
Overall death rates of pipe and cigar smokers are
only slightly higher than among nonsmokers.

4. *Give up smoking, yourself.*
Your arguments against his smoking aren't going
to make headway if you're giving him statistics
between puffs.

5. *Without pushing the point, make him aware that
his welfare is important to you.*
You need your husband. Make this clear, and he will
get your message.

6. *Realize that quitting isn't easy.*
Work with him to find a substitute for smoking.

Here are some habit-changing suggestions: If he reaches

for a cigarette as he gets out of bed in the morning, get up twenty minutes before he does and surprise him with a substitute. Black coffee, maybe, or a vibrator back rub, or an earlier than usual breakfast. And if he associates smoking with a particular activity like typewriting, card playing, reading, or drinking, keep substitute packages of gum beside his typewriter, hard candy on the card table, low-calorie snacks near his cocktail glass. Try to arrange a trip to coincide with his push to quit, or if this is impossible, get his secretary to keep Nikoban or another habit-breaker in his desk at the office. In principle, such panaceas either give pleasure like a cigarette or make the taste of tobacco unappetizing just as certain drugs take away the desire for alcohol.

Excessive drinking and life expectancy

Alcoholism is not given as the cause of death on many death certificates even when heavy drinking is a factor, because of the doctor's deference to the feelings of the deceased person's family. Instead, the cause goes down as cirrhosis of the liver or pneumonia or a fractured skull or suffocation or first-degree burns suffered in an accident on the highway or a home, even though the real cause was uncontrolled drinking.

Authorities say the life expectancy of an excessive drinker is ten to twelve years less than the average, and the Department of Health, Education, and Welfare says that cirrhosis of the liver occurs about eight times as frequently among alcoholics as among others. Alcohol also makes for a lowered sensitivity to pneumonia and other infections. So if your husband is packing away a few more martinis or Scotches every day, he is probably headed for trouble, and if he is a jolly fellow who shies away from hard liquor but drinks great quantities of beer, he may be in even worse shape. Not only will a big intake of beer add to his weight problem, but it is hard on his heart.

Does your husband drink too much?

Of the eighty million adult drinkers in the United States, between six and eight million are alcoholics, or one in fifteen, and more men than women fall into the estimated 5 to 6 percent of our population with this problem. According to Dr. Ruth Fox, president of the American Medical Society on Alcoholism, only a small percentage are skid row derelicts.

"More than 70 percent of today's excessive drinkers," she says, "reside in respectable neighborhoods, live with their wives (or husbands), try to send their children to college, belong to the country club, attend church, pay taxes, and continue to perform more or less effectively as bank presidents, housewives, farmers, salesmen, machinists, stenographers, teachers, clergymen, and physicians."

Chances are if your husband began turning to liquor in his teens as a tranquilizer for feelings of inferiority, he has had to break away from alcohol by now or he is an addicted alcoholic, and you know the symptoms of addiction only too well. But let's say that your husband has shown no signs of addiction until recently after years and years of holding his liquor as well as any other social drinker around. Now you see and are concerned about obvious changes in his behavior, and you wonder what to do. For one thing, don't panic. Unlike neurotic alcoholics who are unable to face everyday difficulties with or without liquor, your husband can once again be on top of life, but he probably will need help to free himself from his craving for alcohol which is now due to underlying physiological factors of tissue tolerance, metabolic changes, and withdrawal phenomena.

Foolproof test of dependency

If you believe your husband has a drinking problem, don't ask him to go on the wagon, which is no test at all. Ask him, instead, to try to stick to an agreed-upon number of drinks (one drink, two drinks, or three drinks a day, but no more than three) every time he drinks in the next six months, no matter what the occasion.* (This does not mean he must drink this amount daily, but he cannot drink more.) If he goes along with your suggestion and can limit himself without expection to a quota determined beforehand, he probably is not an alcoholic; if he cannot, he has definitely lost control. Should your husband fail the test, consult an experienced doctor who will recommend Alcoholics Anonymous or a psychiatrist or group therapy or Antabuse, a medication which interferes with the metabolism of alcohol so that even one drink causes a toxic reaction resulting in vomiting, shock, and a pounding headache.† Once your husband talks to the doctor, you can relax.

Too many for the road

Not all heavy drinkers will become problem drinkers, but at given times all can be problem drivers. Because people with a higher education and income status often are wealthier and entertain more they tend to drink more; thus you and your husband may very easily find yourselves members of a circle of heavy drinkers. If so, watch your intake at

* This do-it-yourself test to determine alcoholism is suggested by Marty Mann, *New Primer on Alcoholism,* New York, Holt, Rinehart & Winston, 1958.
† Never administer Antabuse without your husband's knowledge. It must be given under a doctor's care only, and the decision to use it must come from him and your husband, as must all treatment decisions.

cocktail parties, and if your husband drinks more than usual, *you do the driving.* For it is on the highway that alcohol really takes its toll.*

The man with too much to drink, the Allstate Insurance Company reports, is about twenty-five times more likely to have an accident than when he is sober, and, cites the United States Department of Transportation's report, one driver out of every fifty is drunk. Strangely enough, alcohol is not involved in the accidents of teenagers as often as in the accidents of older drivers, and the worst drunk-driving records belong to men between the ages of twenty-five and forty-four. In later years, when pedestrian-vehicle accidents become a frequent cause of death, one out of three such pedestrians has been drinking heavily. So even though your husband is a fairly cautious fellow who takes no more than an occasional cocktail and, maybe, wine with dinner, he is not safe as either a driver or a stroller because of other drinkers. So what do you do?

1. Drive when your husband has been drinking, and you have not.
2. Drive when your husband is tired, and you are not.
3. Check the drunk-driver laws in your state, and push for the right kind.
4. Keep your seat belts fastened.

Answers to three seat-belt alibis

With a death rate from traffic accidents now close to one hundred deaths a day, the National Safety Council estimates that five thousand lives a year can be saved by using seat

---

* Traffic authorities say that drinking is involved in at least half of the nation's 55,500 traffic deaths each year, and some say alcohol is a factor in as many as 87 percent of the cases.

belts. Here are the three most often heard alibis: (1) I fasten mine for a long trip, but not near home. (2) I use mine when I'm going fast on the highway, but not when I'm in town. (3) I have a horror of being strapped inside a burning car. Answers: (1) Most traffic accidents occur within a few miles of home. (2) Forty-five percent of accidents happen at a speed of less than forty miles per hour. (3) With your belt fastened, you are less apt to be injured and will have a better chance to escape. *Get your husband to buckle up.*

Nondriving accidents

In later years, when both men and women become more accident-prone, falls and burns are more to be feared than motor vehicle accidents. And here you are going to have to watch *your* step. (Female deaths from falls and burns far outnumber male fatalities.) Respect your tendency to fall, and for his sake and yours, go easy.

Your husband needs your love

At a recent statewide "Empty Nest Symposium" in New Britain, Connecticut, Dr. Raul Lopez, of Kensington, talked about the importance of sex in the life of the middle-aged man not only as a release from tension but as evidence of his wife's love. "Love him," he told the women in his audience, saying that certain hormonal changes that take place in the male during the sex act actually work against "artery rusting." Certainly, there is evidence that the happily married man usually outlives the lonely bachelor or widower.

So what's ahead?

Face up to the fact that you may outlive your husband, but don't bore him or yourself by rehearsing for widowhood as some women admit to doing. Take ordinary precautions and be glad that your husband's life expectancy is rosier than his father's.* Recently, there has been a dip, however. So do take care of your husband as recommended here, but, once again, *don't fuss.* Count on long years together in your empty nest and make the most of them.

New findings

Dr. George Gallup, of Princeton, New Jersey, said after studying a large number of men who lived to a ripe old age, "There's one thing about them; they're interested in everything."

Recommendation: Encourage your husband to do what he wants to do whether you're interested or not. And don't insist on too much togetherness; you go your way and let him go his. (If you love bridge and he loves gardening, don't feel guilty about heading for a foursome while he works at home. Or if he likes to sail, and you like to garden, don't feel you ought to be a good wife and push out to sea. Stay with your flowers and wait for him to come in.) Your dinner hour will be all the better for this.

About his work: If he has a high-pressure job and loves it, don't urge his retirement. New findings show that men running huge businesses have no more heart attacks than workers with routine jobs. Let him push.

---

* A baby boy born in 1900 had a life expectancy of 46.3 years; in 1920, 53.6; in 1940, 60.8; in 1965, 66.8. Then, in 1966, according to *Vital Statistics of the United States,* came the first dip. Male life expectancy was estimated at 66.7 years.

Above all, get set for a perked-up marriage. Children who served as a bond may also have been a distraction. Without them, you and your husband can renew a deeply personal relationship. His joy in this relationship, doctors say now, can serve as much as anything else to prolong his life.

3

HEALTH PITFALLS YOU CAN AVOID

With so much talk about vulnerability of the male, many women get to thinking of themselves as indestructible at this age which, of course, is not the case. However, the new empty nester does get a break in that twenty-year heart risk postponement (causing many doctors to believe that specific sex hormones play a part), and she does seem to have a better record in statistical tables all along the way. (Here, again, experts believe the difference is in the sex makeup of each, pointing out that women possess two X chromosomes; men, only one.) Still, as you know from watching your husband handily twist off the cap of a jar which you haven't been able to budge, a woman is not as physically strong as a man. And women are far more prone than men to several diseases.

Female susceptibilities

A woman is more susceptible than a man to disorders of the reproductive tract and the endocrine system. (Her susceptibility to carcinoma of the genitalia is 3 to 1 over his;

carcinoma of the gall bladder, 10 to 1.) She is more susceptible than her husband to arthritis (4 to 1); to hyperthy-
roidism (10 to 1); and to migraine (6 to 1). And there is a
100 percent greater chance that she rather than he will be
anemic. As previously pointed out, she is also more accident
prone than her husband as they both get older.

In Chapter 1 you assessed the present condition of your
health and made a "grocery list" of remedies for everyday
comfort-robbers. Now it's time to take precautions against
more serious possibilities.

To sum up: As a woman, you have a longer life expectancy
than a man of your age, but this does not mean that you are
going to be feeling fit day after day unless you give yourself the same kind of care now that you have always given
to your children and are now giving to your husband.

Take these simple precautions

Go to your family doctor (or a gynecologist) for a breast
and vaginal examination once a year; oftener, if signaled.
When there, report any frequent headaches, joint stiffness,
dizziness, sleeplessness, and/or unusual fatigue.

Take cold and/or flu shots in the fall. (The older you are
the more serious a bug can be.)

For special conditions like anemia, numbness of extremities, and sinus problems, take iron, calcium, and special
vitamins as prescribed.

For menopausal symptoms, *insist* that your doctor consider
estrogen hormones to relieve anxiety, hot flashes, base-of-the-
skull headaches, and tingly hands and feet. It is a rare physician today who refuses to supplement the female's depleted
supply of estrogen with hormone pills when her ovaries
stop producing. But no doctor is going to call up a patient

and tell her to start taking hormones if he doesn't know she's troubled. There is little reason today to go through the menopause as your grandmother did. So *don't suffer in silence*.

Like your husband, go easy on fats, sweets, and cigarettes, and *keep moving*. And should you bump into a real depression, call a psychologist or psychiatrist and not the liquor store.*

What a psychiatrist will tell you

A well-known psychiatrist told me recently that no patient had ever come to him whose worries were not involved in some way with money, sex, or status. If you are abnormally nervous right now, your anxiety may be coming from your changed status in your empty nest. *Does anybody need you any more?*

In the early years of marriage, a husband looks to his wife for encouragement as he ventures into business. By the time he is sailing along fine without a cheer leader, his wife is needed in this role by the children. Ideally, both parents are equally interested in the psychological needs of the children, but in most cases, this becomes pretty much the mother's area as the father turns more and more to filling material needs.

This division of labor makes for a schism about the time

---

* Dr. Fox reports that most authorities now estimate a 1 to 3 ratio of women alcoholics to men alcoholics and says that drinking by women in the middle and upper income group is either markedly on the increase or these women are more willing now than in the past to seek treatment. In her private practice, she now has more women alcoholics than men and believes that the ratio in the upper income group is now 1 to 1 and that women with alcohol problems may actually outnumber men.

the children leave home. A man who concentrates on business affairs for twenty-five years finds more stimulation and excitement in his work at forty-five than ever before. A mother, on the other hand, who does her job well, emancipates her children and finds herself in her forties with no one to cheer.

A graph of the average wife's importance to her husband and/or children peaks in the young married years, then declines steadily until her husband's retirement when it peaks again. Obviously, if a woman has no daily interest when the nest empties, other than her children and housekeeping, she is going to feel depressed at this time when her husband's interest peaks in his career. For the next fifteen or twenty years, he will be functioning away from home at top capacity, and her life is going to be as empty as her nest if she turns to him as her only source of happiness; and she is going to have a long wait if she spends her days looking forward to his retirement. Unless she looks out, she's bound to feel a lack of status.

Happily, opportunities for the vital over-forty woman to travel, go back to school, serve others, and earn money are everywhere. Should you find yourself resisting, talk to an analyst. You may feel guilty about your new freedom; or you may be worried that anything you do can't measure up to your husband's career; or you may be fearful about stepping out of your housewife role. A session or two may be all you need.

How to obtain a psychiatrist

Not long ago the following letter to Ann Landers was printed in her column. Her answer made such good sense to me that I have asked and been given permission to reprint the column and the answer here:

Dear Ann Landers:

You keep advising people to seek psychiatric help. Will you please be more explicit? How does a person go about finding a psychiatrist he can afford? You often say, "Your family doctor can advise you." Mine can't. I told him I was falling apart even though the tests showed no organic illness. When he said, "There's nothing wrong with you," I answered, "Something must be wrong. Maybe I need a psychiatrist." His reply was, "Everybody has problems of one kind or another. Stop worrying and you will be all right."

Frequently you suggest a mental health clinic for those who can't afford private therapy. Where are these clinics? How does one find them? You do a world of good, Ann. Please do a little more by answering my questions.—Counting On You.

Dear Counting:

The physician who told you to "stop worrying" should go back to medical school. At long last they are teaching doctors how to deal with patients whose emotional problems are making them physically ill. Instructing a patient to "stop worrying" makes about as much sense as telling him to stop sweating.

Here is the procedure for those who want the names of Psychiatric Clinics. Look in the phone book under COUNTY Hospital. Or telephone the Community Fund Agency in your city. (In some cities it is called the United Fund.) Larger cities have a Community Referral Service which can direct you. (In Chicago, the Community Referral is superb. Telephone RA 6-0363.)

Free clinics are usually found at universities. A phone call to the university will tell you what services are available. People who live in small towns should telephone the County Medical Society in the nearest large city.

Anyone who wishes detailed information should write to the National Association for

Mental Health in New York. The address is 10 Columbus Circle, New York, N.Y. 10019. Those who wish private psychiatric care should ask their physicians. And I hope to heaven they receive a better answer than you did.

Fat in the head and hips

Boredom (or a feeling of self-consciousness or inadequacy) makes for fat. Stay home, alone, all day, when there isn't enough there to do, and you're going to compensate for your uninteresting life by eating or drinking or spending passive, unselective hours in front of TV, all of which will widen your hips and fatten your head. Lone snacking, lone drinking, and lone viewing are insidious in that in the doing they are invisible. But their effects become apparent soon enough—first to a husband and then to others. Soon the extra pounds or the alcoholism and the terrible dullness tend to intensify the very condition that led to the problem in the first place.

Few husbands are proud of overweight wives and few stay with an alcoholic one.* And the husband who has been wheeling and dealing in the business world all day is hardly stimulated at night by the woman who has been watching one television game show after another. So, if you have a tendency to nibble, nip, or sit during daytime hours, break the habit with this simple recipe. (1) Winter, summer, rain or shine, get out and away from the house for at least two hours a day. (2) Talk to three different people (no fair counting people like the oil man) a day about something interesting that you have been doing or thinking about.

---

* For every ten wives who stay with an alcoholic husband, only one husband stays with an alcoholic wife.

(3) When you feel sorry for yourself, do something for a child with a problem.*

Your husband pays more attention than you think

Your adjustment to life in an empty nest is a preview for your husband of what he will be going through when he retires. So even though he may say little about what you do every day, he is getting insight into himself as he watches you. Also, as he gets to know you and see you again without the children, he begins to formulate a plan for the rest of your lives together. The more stimulated you are about life around you, the happier he is going to be in the long run, even though what you seem to be doing has little to do with him. You are his hope and his promise for the years coming up. Show him by keeping yourself physically and psychologically fit that life is far from over and that empty nest living (before and after retirement) can be the most fun yet.

---

* As a foster grandparent to a handicapped child or as a volunteer working with disadvantaged children through Head Start, you will learn firsthand that a child can be happy even when there seems little reason to be. *Take note!*

4

HOW TO GET RID OF FATTY SPOTS BY THINKING LEAN

If you are fifteen or twenty pounds overweight, you have fatty places in the stomach area, buttocks, and around your shoulder blades. Put on a snug girdle and bra or a two-piece bathing suit, and fat puffs up around your abdomen and over your bra in the back. Now, by programming your brain as a scientist feeds a computer, you can get rid of this embarrassing fat in less than six weeks.

Besides this book, here is all you need

1. A snug girdle (or skimpy underpants) and bra (or a two-piece bathing suit)
2. A full-length mirror
3. A desire to eliminate fatty spots
4. Two minutes morning and night for dedicated scrutiny
5. A 6 by 2 1/2 foot plywood board (3/4 inch thick)

6. A belief in the power of the subconscious mind
7. Ten minutes a night for mental programming on your slant board

Ready?

Before going to bed tonight, inspect yourself in a full-length mirror in your girdle and bra or two-piece suit.* For at least two minutes look at yourself from all angles. In profile, does your stomach protrude? Is there a roll of fat around your middle? Another roll pushed up from under your arms in the back? Does your rear end stick out? *Don't turn away*. Register in your mind a picture of the fatty places you want to get rid of.

Get set

After inspection, get ready for bed as usual (bathe, brush your teeth, cream your face, pin curl your bangs, etc.). Last thing, before lying on your slant board, read how to program your mind. (If you do not have a board tonight, lie in bed when doing your programming with a pillow under your hips and two pillows under your feet. Tomorrow, buy the plywood board and keep it under your bed. To slant, simply prop one end up on a footstool or the side of your bed.) Always lie on your back with your head down, feet up.

---

* Wear this same girdle and bra or two-piece suit each night and morning for mirror study. No fair inspecting yourself in a slip or in the nude. It's that bunched-up fat you must become aware of.

Read these instructions before lying down

In a room, alone, concentrate on one word—*elegant*. See the word: *elegant*. Spell it: E L E G A N T. Now spell the word five times with your eyes closed. Look at the word again—*elegant*.

Read this next aloud. "When I lie down, I will see elegant clothes: a beautifully cut dress by Adele Simpson, I. Miller shoes, a crocodile handbag, white boots, soft French gloves, a slim diamond bracelet. I will see elegant furnishings: a patterned-silk Louis XVI chair, a crystal chandelier, flowers in a Steuben bowl, a thick Chinese rug. And elegant men: John Lindsay, Eric Sevareid, Fred Astaire. My own ideas of elegance: real lace, cut crystal, a painting by John Singer Sargent. I will hear a Chopin nocturne, see a graceful stairway. Every time the pictures stop, I will spell the word E L E G A N T until they begin again."

Go to sleep after your programming, and chances are your dreams will bring more images.

Go

Set your alarm for ten minutes from now, and don't let yourself be interrupted until the bell rings, no matter what. Turn out the light. Lie on your slant board. Go! E L E-G A N T!

Tomorrow morning, inspect yourself in your girdle and bra, noting fatty spots. Spell the word: E L E G A N T. Go about your day as planned.

Following are instructions for the next six nights. Do not read now. Turn immediately to page 40—but come back to this page for directions for tomorrow and subsequent nights.

Second night

After mirror inspection and bedtime preparation, think of one word—*vital*. See the word: *vital*. Spell it: V I T A L —once, twice . . . five times. Program your mind with pictures of foods you must eat daily to maintain vitality.

Memorize this statement: "Every day I will have two glasses of nonfat milk or buttermilk or some cottage cheese, yogurt, or soup made with milk. Also, I will eat toast or cereal and an orange, tomato, or half a grapefruit. I will eat a piece of broiled chicken, broiled fish, or lean beef and sometimes an egg, and cabbage or lettuce salad, and other vegetables like celery, radishes, green peppers, beans, spinach, mushrooms, broccoli, asparagus. And, always, I will keep plenty of fruit in the house: apples, nectarines, peaches, oranges, lemons, apricots, raisins, pears."

You *must* know the above words by heart. So, say them over and over again. When you lie with eyes closed on your slant board, see yourself shopping at your market for the food you must have every day. Say the memorized words as you see yourself putting your food away at home. Last of all, picture yourself arranging a beautiful bowl of fruit as you spell the word: V I T A L.

Set your alarm for ten minutes from now, turn out the light and begin: V I T A L. Go to sleep, dream, and tomorrow morning inspect yourself as usual in your two-piece suit and go on with your day.

Third night

When ready for bed after mirror inspection, concentrate on *vigor*. See the word: *vigor*. Spell it: V I G O R—once, twice . . . five times.

Read this paragraph aloud before setting your alarm for your slant-board programming. "I will think tonight of everything I do (or have ever done) that makes me feel vigorous. Swimming, running, walking, golfing, sailing, jogging, exercising, or hurrying up and down stairs. As I relax, I will fill my mind with pictures of vigorous people in action. Ethel Kennedy playing tennis, a great skier like Jean-Claude Killy whizzing down a slope, Olympic chamion Peggy Fleming figure skating, Joe DiMaggio hitting a baseball. Finally, I will feel myself diving in perfect form, driving a golf ball, batting a baseball, serving on a tennis cour'. I will feel myself skimming down a snowy hill on a sled, running in the wind. Every time the pictures cease, I will spell the word again: V I G O R."

As you go to sleep after ten minutes on your slant board, again spell *vigor:* V I G O R.

When you make your mirror inspection in your girdle and bra the next morning, note your fatty spots as usual, but see yourself, too, as you *can* look, tall and slim in a black leotard. Spell V I G O R before eating the breakfast you know you should have.

Fourth night

As you turn and move as you will when fatty spots are gone, hold in your mind's eye Botticelli's famous painting, "The Birth of Venus" (nude on sea shell). After inspection, concentrate on the word *slim*. Spell it: S L I M—once, twice . . . five times. Then read this paragraph aloud.

"On the slant board with my eyes closed, I will see myself say no to a cinnamon roll, a waffle, gravy on potatoes, peanut butter on bread, mayonnaise on salad, a glass of beer, a sweet soft drink, a second drink of anything, a piece of juicy pie, a gooey piece of cake, a piece of my favorite candy. I will, then, select the most attractive slim woman I can think of—Audrey Hepburn, Aline Saarinen, Arlene Francis, Katherine Hepburn, Lena Horne, Barbara Walters, Joan Kennedy, Pat Nixon—you name her, and see myself having lunch with her. I will see her order a light lunch, and I will order the same, and we will talk and eat. I will see us get up together and walk away from the table. In my mind, I will be as slim as my companion."

Spell the word *slim* to yourself as you go to sleep, and in the morning inspect yourself again in the nude, seeing not Venus this time, but *you,* tall and proud and slim.

Fifth night

Do your mirror inspection in your girdle and bra again tonight and study fatty spots that you know now will go. Then, concentrate on the word *active.*

See the word: *active.* Spell it: A C T I V E, five times. Say it again and again and when you lie down, see yourself eating everything you need at breakfast, lunch, and dinner tomorrow to maintain the vigor to do all you want to do. Then, see yourself doing tomorrow's chores with delight. See yourself waving happily to friends as you drive your car, go shopping, arrange a bridge game, plan a trip to a play or movie, make a date with your grandchildren, sign up for a painting lesson. And just before you get up from the board, make a definite plan to begin one project tomorrow you have been putting off. Smile to yourself at how easy this postponed project is going to be.

Tonight, before going to sleep, write down this plan in your notebook. This can be as simple as to sign up for a swimming class, invite three to play bridge later in the week, invite six for dinner next week, arrange a weekend trip. After writing this down, spell the word, A C T I V E, and go to sleep.

In the morning, for the first time, dress before your two-minute inspection and, then, begin immediately to follow through on last night's plan. Spell A C T I V E as you begin.

Sixth night

Forget your girdle and bra and do all inspection in the nude from now on unless otherwise directed. But now stand on a scale for two minutes in front of the mirror night and morning as you check the disappearance of fat.

Chances are if you weighed yourself a week ago, you have lost a pound. Check your weight now, anyway, so that you can enjoy the loss of the pounds that are about to go. And tonight concentrate on the word *joy*. See the word: *joy*. Spell it: J O Y. Say it over and over again to yourself: *joy*.

On your slant board think of the greatest joys you have known in life. Joy that came from accomplishment or relief or delight in another's joy. Think of the five persons you know best. (Your husband, probably, and four others.) What will give each one the joy that he or she seeks? Can you help? If not, you can make a wish (or pray) that each one will receive what will bring the joy you know each one is seeking. See that person experiencing joy, and sharing that joy with you.

For your personal joy, as a starter, see yourself with no fatty spots, tall and slim and attractive. Know that this loss of weight, and the self-indulgence that goes with it, will change your life for the better.

Before you go to sleep, spell J O Y. Next morning, during

mirror inspection, think of all the happy things that you can count on for this day. Eat breakfast with your husband, if possible. Smile as you get ready: joy.

Seventh night

This night, after mirror inspection, concentrate on the word *me*. M E. No need to spell it over and over because we're talking about you.

Think of all that you know about yourself physically. What can't you eat or drink without having a bad reaction? What extra vitamins, minerals, chemicals, does your body need? After what kind of a day does fatigue set in? Do you have frequent headaches? Are you often constipated? What brings relief? What are your physical strong points? What are your weaknesses? How much sleep do you need? Are you a morning or a night person? A hot weather person or a woman for all seasons? What climate is best for you? Are you the nervous type? How do you react in emergency? Are you physically passive or active by nature?

On your slant board, think of how a doctor would prescribe for you if he knew about you what you know. Decide how much exercise you need and what kind you enjoy (walking, swimming, doing housework, or a competitive sport). What foods should you shy away from? What are you allergic to? What can you substitute for the needed foods that do not appeal to you? Do you dislike being alone? How can you find the companionship you crave? Or are your days filled with people whom you really dislike? How can you avoid these people? Are you doing work you like? See your solutions tonight. See yourself in an environment that will promote your psychological and physical health. And when your alarm signals stop, do not get up. Stay on your board and work out a blended health recipe that will give you everything your special body chemistry requires. See yourself putting nonfat dry milk and water into your blender along with every vitamin, protein, and prescribed mineral that you know is needed by your body.*

After you formulate and see yourself blending your personal recipe, repeat these words to yourself in bed before going to sleep: *elegant, vital, vigorous, slim, active, joy, me!*

Because it has taken years for you to add fat, you won't lose all spots the first week—so go back to page 34 and go right through each day's programming again. If you are no more than twenty pounds overweight, by one week from tonight you will have lost two pounds and from then on the going will be easy.

Why this program works

For every 3,500 calories you take in but do not use, you gain about a pound. So if you have fatty spots, you have been eating far more than you need. Once your mind is conditioned to reject foods loaded with calories† that you can't possibly use, you will store up no more fat, so obviously you

---

* Recipe at our house: Each morning I blend 2 calcium wafers, 2 capsules of Vitamin E (which I know from working with Ray Anderson, Doctor of Chemistry, General Mills Research, has a positive effect on every cell in your body), 2 envelopes of unflavored gelatin, 2/3 cup nonfat dry milk, a peeled lemon, and 1 tbs. honey (or a peeled orange and 1 tbs. molasses), and enough ice cold spring water from our tap to fill two ten-inch glasses. (I take a hormone pill with my drink; my husband does not.) Cost per glass is about the same as a soft drink and calorie content is less than two hundred calories per glass. In the summer (and in winter, if we're in the south), we swim before a light breakfast of toast and coffee which is all we want because after the concoction I whip up, we're full.

† If you have only a sketchy knowledge of the caloric content of basic foods, send twenty-five cents to the Superintendent of Documents, U.S. Government Printing Office, Washington, D.C. 20402, for "Calories and Weights" (USDA Pocket Guide), Home and Garden Bulletin No. 153.

will not gain. And soon you will begin to lose. As you turn to vitality-boosting foods rather than the fat-makers, you will just naturally move around and burn up more fuel. When this happens, your body will begin to consume its own stored-up fat, and unsightly fatty spots will go.

You will have no scrawny neck, no flabby arms, no sagging breasts, and no wrinkled face with this program because you will be consuming necessary vitamins, minerals, and proteins that prevent withering. Along with this, your gravity-defying sessions on your slant board will increase circulation to your face and bring relief to sagging muscles.

To be expected: a surging interest in clothes

As you move along in your vitality-boosting program, you will become gloriously aware of your body, and this new awareness will lead quite naturally to a new interest in clothes. Now, perhaps, for the first time in years, you will experience a sensual feeling of well-being when you wear something you like. This will have nothing to do with the effect of your clothes on anyone else. Your feeling of pleasure will be a purely personal reaction to the psychological and physical comfort you gain from wearing clothes that truly please *you*.

The surest test of how you feel about yourself as a woman, say psychologists, is the degree of sensual enjoyment you get from what you wear. This feeling has nothing to do with what you pay for your clothes, nor even with your being clean and well groomed. You can get out of a bathtub, give yourself a manicure, have your hair done, and put on a new expensive dress, and you still may not experience the sensual delight in your body that we are talking about here.

If you have never known this feeling, you have a treat

coming. Joy in your woman power is your birthright, and it will come as you proceed with the energy-expanding program described in this chapter, and as your good taste gets a chance to reveal itself through recommendations given in the next section. As you become healthier and more fashion-conscious, you are bound to look and feel more attractive in everything you wear.

As a prelude to a prettier you, go through your closets and drawers and get rid of everything you ever wear that doesn't make you feel well dressed and stylish. "It is better," say fashion experts, "to have one outfit that you know looks great on you than many costumes that you're not sure about." Pare down, so that later you can quietly build up.

Go to fashion shows sponsored by women's organizations and in local department stores. Subscribe to one good fashion magazine and look through others when you are under the dryer in a beauty shop. As you pay more attention to fashion, you will become increasingly aware that it is the cut of a dress, the hang of it, the easy swing that makes for distinction, not the glittery pin, the bows, and the tricky buttons. Soon you will recognize the identifying marks of good design in a dress just as an art expert sees the marks of worth in a painting. When this happens you will be glad to be rid of the clothes that you felt just so-so about, because your new clothes are going to be sensational.

Vital, busy women who do things have to be well turned out always, so the clothes, shoes, hats, wigs, everything they own must be pretty, packable, and easy to maintain. Thus, everything they wear is simple.

Look for easy-moving, beautifully cut clothes without doodads. You may pay more per dress, but your overall wardrobe will be less expensive than when you were buying one thing after another for every occasion that came along. Now, even though you may have only three or four dresses in your closet, you will feel well dressed wherever you go.

Never again need you feel vaguely dissatisfied with anything you put on. As a result of your new selectivity, every dress you own will look right, and because of your pride in your vital, slimmed-down body, every dress will feel right. Once you know this feeling, you will not have to worry that your extra poundage and old over-the-hill attitudes will return. You will be far too pleased with the new you to let yourself slip.

Old habits go deep

For several days or even weeks when you first start your "think lean" program, your subconscious mind which has turned to food for years for relief from tension may reject your conscious desire to slim down. Go on as directed and don't worry about your continued temptation to snack and overeat. This craving will go, but if you care to hurry this plan along, here are simple food-resisting aids to help your body get used to fewer calories:*

1. Keep a plastic bag of nonfattening foods like celery, radishes, carrot sticks in your refrigerator.
2. Keep a percolator of caffeine-free coffee bubbling away all the time. Drinking this won't "hype" you up, but it will give you oral satisfaction.
3. Do something like walking or swimming (or some other physical exercise) when you feel the urge to eat. This will ease nervousness and help you use up unused fat.
4. Resist alcoholic beverages. A small martini adds two hundred calories.†
5. Never stand up and eat. When you feel yourself put-

---

* When you begin losing one or two pounds a week, you can be sure (even without counting) that you are cutting from five hundred to one thousand calories out of your daily diet and even more if you have recently been putting on weight.
† Also, alcohol gives one a bloated look. Give it up, and you immediately will look thinner.

ting a cracker or cookie in your mouth, sit down as
if you were going to eat a meal.

6. Get your hair shaped or cut now for the attractive
    person you will soon become. Experiment with
    makeup.

7. Brush your teeth after eating anything. (Then, eat-
    ing a potato chip or any other snacking simply won't
    be worth the trouble.)

Suppose you and your husband are way overweight

As you condition your mind to select vitality boosters and
reject fat makers, you will automatically buy and serve foods
that will help your husband as well as you to cut down. But
if either of you is more than twenty pounds overweight,
you probably eat compulsively and have been overweight for
years. To change your daily habits drastically, you need help
from a doctor, weight reduction clinic,* psychiatrist (or all
three), or the encouragement of other dieters in your same
boat.

Like Alcoholics Anonymous, Weight Watchers, TOPS
(Take Off Pounds Sensibly), and Jean Seltzer's Weight
Control, Inc., are organizations dedicated to changing the
daily habits of members through mutual support. Mrs.
Seltzer, who has a summer place a few miles from us,
weighed 166 pounds and wore a size twenty dress six years
ago; she is now a lean size nine. (For five years she has
maintained her weight at 122 pounds.) In her classes she
doesn't talk about will power or self-control, but about
courage. "We're a courage bank. When you have some, you
give a little. When you need some, you draw a little out."
If you are fat and need this kind of encouragement, call

* At the Mayo Clinic at Rochester, Minnesota, wives are given nutri-
tional instruction as part of their husband's weight-reduction plan.

Weight Watchers, Weight Control, Inc., the YWCA, TOPS, or a church group now. If your husband is overweight, encourage him to join a weight-reduction group with you. If he is self-conscious about this, don't insist, but do serve meals that will help you both become and stay slim. Once you are down to your desired weight, begin your nightly slant-board conditioning described earlier for women with less to lose.

5

SEX WHEN YOU'RE OVER FIFTY

In your early married years, back before the pill, most of your friends, and probably you, had three or at least two children. Now that your last one, born about the time you were twenty-seven, is living away from home, you probably have reached the menopause period. Far from finding this physical change the nervous disaster you have been led to believe, you feel fine most of the time. Unlike your grandmother who had no vitamin shots, hormone additives, or tension aids (and was depleted, perhaps, by years of hard work and excessive childbearing), you are more attractive than you were when the children were home. And married to a vigorous man who is enjoying his work as never before, you *love* this time of life. Your sex life, say psychiatrists and doctors, should and probably does reflect this.

A woman who appreciates and admires her husband and feels secure in her relationship with him can give herself to him sexually in the empty nest years with the same (or more) psychic energy than before. Released from the fear of conception and freed from distracting worries about the children and money, psychiatrists say, she can turn her attention to her husband as she did when she was a bride. There will, however, be some specific differences in the sex act itself. For instance, one doctor told me, "A woman after menopause reacts a little more slowly to erotic stimuli than before." Not all medical authorities agree, but many interested in the problems of this particular group say that women may become self-conscious during intercourse at this age due to a belief that they *have to perform*. According to Dr. William H. Masters, director of the Reproductive Biology Research Foundation in St. Louis, "Many women don't have the need for orgasmic expression every time they're mounted. Still, such women enjoy intercourse thoroughly and are satisfied if not satiated."

There is also a diminishing urge on the part of the male as he gets older to have orgasm, say Dr. Masters and his assistant, Mrs. Virginia Johnson, authors of the book, *Human Sexual Response*. According to these authorities, many men lapse into sexual inactivity because of the diminishing urge for orgasm, although erection persists more often than not into old age. Dr. Masters encourages men to appreciate the pleasure they find in nonorgasmic sex which also gives pleasure to their wives.

Not harmful to men

One persistent belief keeps some women from encouraging intercourse in their over-fifty husbands. Many wives have the idea that the physical exertion called for in the sex act may actually be harmful to middle-aged men. This is far from true. According to Dr. Raul Lopez, heart specialist, who admonishes wives to "stop picking on your husbands when they come home tired from the office and give them plenty of love, instead"; the sex act produces two hormones in a man's body which do remarkable things "for extending his life." Dr. Lopez advises wives of his male patients to make love with their husbands "on a fairly regular basis," pointing out that, among other things, hormones produced during the sex act decrease lipides in the man's blood stream.

"A long and happy marriage is a definite factor in a man's longevity," is the conclusion of Dr. Lopez and of others who have researched the subject. And, certainly, we know that married men outlive bachelors, not just because sex on a regular basis works to prevent "artery rusting," but because a happily married man has a feeling of being cared for, has a sympathetic friend to come home to after a long, tough day.

Dr. Robert Collier Page, internationally known expert in occupational health, whose book *How to Lick Executive Stress* differentiates between horizontal (sick) and vertical (healthy) living, tells wives to let their husbands talk "for the first fifteen or twenty minutes after they get home. By that time, they'll relax, and be more than willing to listen to whatever you want to talk about." Experts say that talking out the day's problems with a person committed to helping you work out your problems, whatever they may be, is an act of faith—and this faith, or love, liberates sexuality.

As prevalent as the belief that the sex act is harmful to the middle-aged male is the myth that there are more divorces after the children leave than before. Not true. More divorces occur before one of the partners is twenty-five years of age than at any other time, and the divorce rate goes down each year following that period. When a divorce does occur after twenty-five or thirty years of marriage, friends are shocked; much discussion takes place. Because of all of the attention given to one or two broken marriages in a given circle, we get the feeling that divorce is the rule in middle-aged couples. Not true, although it is true that many husbands and wives have drifted apart by this age and must make a conscious effort to remember how they once related to each other.

The time for intimacy

Dr. John W. Hudson, sociology professor at Arizona State University and a well-known marriage counselor, says that in the empty-nest period "there is time to reestablish a special kind of intimacy and companionship not possible in the child-rearing years of marriage." He has specific advice for the wife who is worried about reestablishing a close relationship with her husband whose interests may have turned almost totally to business and even, at some time in the past, turned to another woman for the attention and encouragement he may not have been finding at home. "The idea, 'I can't be happy unless,' can be rethought as, 'I will be happy because.' The point is to accept life at the moment—and accept the fact that it will be changing at the next moment, for it will be different then." He encourages wives not to view life in a rear-view mirror but to live right now. Adults tend to become overly cautious, forget life is a risk.

"If an infant held the philosophy of adults," he said when we were in Arizona not long ago, "he would probably never leave the crib, or while learning to walk, would give up after one try." It is Dr. Hudson's belief that we are inclined to become less courageous as we get older. "All along the way, life is made of mistakes, work, practice, and more mistakes. Just because you are no longer in your twenties doesn't mean that you no longer have to face these things."

Certainly, a woman needs to trust the man she gives herself to sexually, whether she has been married to him twenty-five years or one.

Dr. Alexander Lowen, writing with Robert Levin in *Reader's Digest*, made this statement: "We cannot command our body to ignore the deepest truth it knows—that in opening itself to the possibility of pleasure, it stands exposed to the possibility of pain. Furthermore, in the center of our being we are sharply aware that the greater the pleasure we enjoy today, the greater the pain we will suffer tomorrow if we lose the person who gives us pleasure. . . . With love, with the feeling of total commitment, the body in middle age, as in youth, surrenders itself to the pleasure of the moment. . . . Thus," says Dr. Lowen, "love liberates sexuality, enabling us to accept our own sense of physical joy; and that joy in turn enriches our love."

While all authorities agree that a woman's need for her husband's assurance of love is not as fierce in middle age as it is in youth, still, because her self-esteem may be at low ebb when the children leave, her morale gets a boost from assurance of his affection. Unfortunately, if she clings to him in despair, she may find that she is asking for more than he, or anyone, can give.

The best course for a woman, say psychologists, is to look for trust and expect love from her marriage partner of many years, but, at the same time, to pursue interests of her own just as he is pursuing interests of his own. Or as Dr. Lowen puts it, "The pleasure of the sexual embrace on the part of both partners, together with the certainty that they will embrace again, gives them new strength to stand alone." This feeling of harmony is even more appreciated by mature partners than by the very young. It is reflected in everything they do, apart and together, away from and in their homes, away from and in their bedrooms.

The two-way sex stimulant that cannot be denied

Fortunes have been made by peddlers of creams, potions, mechanical vibrators, and other supposed aphrodisiacs, but according to doctors and psychologists there is a simple recipe for a satisfying sex life at any age which far exceeds artificial excitants. It consists of two ingredients: (1) genuine affection of each partner for the other; (2) an individual sense of psychological and physical well-being in each partner. Put another way by Dr. Josephine Ross, our psychologist friend at the Housatonic Psychiatric Center, "Two well-adjusted persons who love each other seldom come to a psychotherapist with sex problems."

Here is a commonsense recommendation: Consistently express your affection in little ways, giving verbal and nonverbal assurances of love. And pay attention to everyday physical rules, too. Without being a fanatic, take good care of your body. With this recipe, your sex life can be satisfying for far longer than was once thought to be true. One study, recently reported by Ruth Winter in *Reader's Digest,* found that 70 percent of healthy, married men and women are sexually active until past seventy. Many years from now, with true affection at the root of the marriage relationship, and reasonable physical health at the foundation of everyday life, the absence of actual intercourse will be hardly noticed or missed. Other expressions of love will be there to take its place.

6

GOOD HEALTH IS CATCHING

Remember in *The Odd Couple* how each member of the twosome picked up neurotic tics and twitches from exposure to the other? We laughed because this is a truth we recognize. Live with another long enough, and you will adopt his facial expressions, voice inflections, even his physical infirmities.

"Live with a lame man," said Plutarch, "and you will learn to halt." Unfortunately for the long married, poor health is catching; fortunately, so is good health.

Don't talk to your husband about minor discomforts

My husband and I once lived next door to a childless, long-married couple whose conversation was completely filled with allusions to the minor discomforts of both. "How are you today?" we would ask one or the other by way of greeting and, then, be sorry.

"When Pam woke up this morning," Henry would tell us, "she had a little stomachache, but she took some Milk of Magnesia and now . . ." Later, Pam would tell us that "Last night Henry got a sliver in his finger but I got it out with a hot needle and . . ." Each one's preoccupation with disability had infected the other until their life contained awareness of nothing much but little pains.

Marriage is the most intimate of all relationships. Thus, small worries and self-doubts are bound to come out, and these confessions, as a sign of mutual trust, are good. But when requests for reassurance emerge as a constant stream of physical complaints, a halt is called for. If you notice such a habit building up at your house, check yourself. You may be acquiring the habit of negativism without realizing it.

How to break the let's-both-complain habit

Without ever mentioning to your husband that you are aware of a growing tendency for both of you to discuss physical discomforts, determine to break this habit now with this easy seven-point plan:

1. Refrain from discussing minor personal complaints of any kind.

2. Suggest a specific solution for any minor discomfort your husband mentions and then stop discussing it. If he brings it up again, suggest action again, but don't cluck, cluck.

3. Do not pacify him with "I'm sure there's nothing the matter," when he confesses a major fear. Call a doctor. If his problem is serious, you will know; if not, you can stop talking about it.

4. Stay away from the woebegone. As you make out a guest list, forget what people you "owe." Invite the doers to your dinner table; skip the complainers.

5. Work more activity into your daily regime. Swim together when you can, take walks together, skate or play golf. You don't have time to think about a

pimple on your ear when you're driving down the fairway.

6. Don't fill your dinner conversation with negative news of sickness, obituaries, robberies, and murder.

7. Through the subtle use of cosmetics, glow like a woman in love! Sitting across the table from a radiant woman will take your husband's mind off his little ills.

Remember, good health is infectious. Court vitality, and your husband will be vital, too.

7

FOR THE MOTHER ALONE: A VITALITY-BOOSTING PROGRAM

Close to eight million graduate mothers live in nests without husbands. Some divorcées and widows live with a friend; a few live with their children; many live alone. Not all of these divorced or widowed women without partners want to remarry. "Get married again?" one woman said when I asked about this. "Why, I've been married." But all admit that living without a man has social drawbacks. "When my husband was living," a New Haven widow told me, "my social life was built in. Today, I have to arrange gatherings that used to just happen."

The mature woman living alone has the same physical concerns as the married empty nester, so everything written here for a wife applies to her, too. But the emotional climate of her home is different. In some ways she has more freedom than her married friends; in other ways, she is more restricted. But one thing is sure: with radiant health and an outgoing nature she can have a satisfying, event-packed life.

Time to discard the old single-woman taboos

Married hostesses used to throw up their hands at the thought of having to produce a single man to "balance off" a single woman. Now they don't feel the need! In this era of casual entertaining, few hostesses care if there is an extra woman or two at her table (which there probably will be) if these women contribute something to the other guests. In fact, they go out of their way to invite dynamic women who are "doing things." (Bette Davis, living nearby in Westport, Connecticut, has no problem keeping her calendar full.)

If you are single, don't feel that you will be a fifth wheel at a party for couples, but do know you will have to give more than a married woman. On an off-night she can depend on her husband to be the outgoing one. You are on your own.

Don't expect to be invited to other homes unless you put out the welcome mat, and when you eat out, pick up the tab when it's your turn. (At a restaurant, ask the headwaiter beforehand to let you pay away from the table.) There's no reason to limit your life to women only, but be realistic about your social responsibilities when traveling in mixed company.

Aunty Queen's vitality formula

My over-eighty Cedar Rapids aunt who has lived alone for thirty years is lovely to look at, maintains her two-floor home easily and well, and has a social calendar that is fuller than mine. Recently, a doctor asked Aunty Queen how many times a day she goes up and down the stairs. "About twenty-five," she said; and he said to me, "I wouldn't change a step of her life for anything in the world."

Her vitality-boosting formula consists of three "keeps":

keep things up, keep up on things, keep going! The formula is foolproof for women who live alone and like it, and for those who want to get married too.

If you want to remarry

There are fewer men than women at your age, but still there are close to four million widowed and divorced men in the United States, many of whom will be walking down the aisle this year with a woman your age. Remember, there are more remarriages for both men and women after forty-five than before. So head up, if you want to marry, keep yourself radiantly healthy and go where men go, and give out, give out, give out. If a man has any sense, you won't be single long.

PART TWO

HAPPINESS IS A HOME THAT SUITS YOU

8

NOW YOU CAN LIVE ANY WAY YOU LIKE

At empty-nest symposiums that I have conducted in various parts of the country, the second question put to me by women is always the same, "Now that the children are gone, shall we move?"* My answer: "If you ask the question at all, the answer is probably yes."

With a paycheck (or two) fatter than ever before and college bills no longer taking a bite, this is the best time for most couples to plan a more glamorous way of life. Yet surprisingly few people move at this age. Sixty-nine percent own their own homes already and have little inclination to switch, often because it's too much bother.

Deck-clearing time

Psychologists say that when the last child says goodbye is the best time in a lifetime for home-assessment. "Clear the decks, and get on with things," they say. Yet they do not

---

* The first question was discussed in Part One, "How can I prolong my husband's life?"

advise moving just for the sake of moving. "But even that is better," one sociologist said, "than to think of childlessness as the end of things and decide to sit out the rest of the show. That can be a long, dull sit." If you have decided to stay put, is this due to love for your home or apathy? Determine this now, and act accordingly.

Lesson to be learned from the astronauts

When Neil Armstrong stepped out on the moon, he carried with him a man-made environment that was exactly right for him. In this custom-fashioned physical and psychological setup he was completely comfortable even in an alien world. Take a lesson from the astronauts.

Analyze what environmental factors make for your comfort or discomfort. Then see to it that you produce the physical and psychological habitat that allows you to function at your optimum wherever you happen to be. Because you spend more time in your home than anywhere else, your first aim should naturally be to work out an environment in the house you live in that is completely right for you.

Comfort is different from habit

My husband and I live in a large country home with sleeping, living, and eating areas on three separate levels. We love every inch of it, but I realized when visiting a friend in a new-style duplex condominium apartment the other day that I lack one comfort giver that she takes for granted. My washer and dryer are two levels down from our bedroom, bath, and upstairs sitting room, where most of our laundry comes from. Her laundry facilities are upstairs in a pullman closet at one end of her bath. "How brilliant!" I heard myself saying.

Would I move just to have an upstairs washer and dryer? No, but after seeing her home I can't kid myself that our home is the most comfortable one we could find. We may stay where we are out of habit; but should we move, I am sure that our next place can be just as comfortable as our friend's if not more so. Far more often than not, staying put is due to a lack of drive, not to a positive decision that this is best for us.

Questions about your home

1. Is it easy for you to keep up, inside and out?
2. Is the temperature right for you at all times? (Warm in winter? Cool in summer?)
3. Is it filled with beautiful and/or meaningful things?
4. Is your bedroom comfortable in every detail?
5. Do you have your own bathroom with a separate one for your mate and/or guests?
6. Can you put up overnight guests without churning things up too much?
7. Does your home have plenty of drawer, closet, and storage space?
8. Do you have a desk, filing place, or maybe a study that is respected as yours?
9. Is the outside of your home or apartment as handsome as the inside? Can you work there with growing things should you desire, or swim, or play croquet or tennis.
10. Can you live in your present neighborhood without fear?

11. Are you close enough to swimming, golf, adult education classes, a good shopping center, friends to play bridge with, etc., to avoid a feeling of isolation?
12. Can you afford to live here about as you live now for the rest of your life no matter what happens?
Count your yes answers.

If you have more than ten yes answers, your home is a joy, but this does not mean that you will never move. Having created the ideal environment for you in one place, you can do so in another. However, if you stay where you are, you will be staying because you prefer living as you live to another way of life, not because resistance to change holds you back.

East or west, is home best?

You may not live in an English castle, a Palm Beach mansion, or a Greek island paradise, but are you proud to take people to your home? And when you return from a vacation and close the door behind you, do you feel in your bones, This is where I belong? The presence or absence of this feeling is your criterion of the suitability of your home environment.

If there's truly no place like home for you, you belong where you are, but remember: you do not have to live exactly as you lived when the children were home. At first you may be conscious of a void. Spread out and your life will be enriched. This section will show you how.

On the other hand, if you feel dissatisfaction in your present setup, you won't experience a change for the better in your present situation as time goes on. The place for you to live is somewhere else; as you read on, you will find suggestions.

9

THE END OF AN ERA
AND A NEW BEGINNING

You may feel a small pang when you come across your daughter's worn ballet slippers or your son's ice skates in the old house, but your compensation can be a home that reflects you and your husband as never before. So except for books and games and a few sentimental dolls and toys, which you can box up for your grandchildren, give away all the things the children left behind. Cling to the past and you will be lonely; start something new and you will be stimulated. The time for a change is now.

As a start, assume for at least one day that you are going to stay in your present home forever, and take a look around. Make notes as you go from room to room. Is there need anymore for that big scratched desk, the old record player, the popcorn popper, that vanity with its rose decals? . . . and what about the old dining room set you got when you moved into this house, the davenport that's had years of wear, the big bookcase containing that old set of encyclopedias? If there is the tiniest question in your mind about whether you should keep something or forget it, *let it go*. Once you feel indifferent, *comme ci comme ça,* about something, you will never like it again!

Sell things you no longer need at a private tag sale or donate them to the Salvation Army, Goodwill Industries, or your favorite charity, church, or thrift shop.* Your husband may be a little amazed when he comes home after the sweep out, but soon he will like the uncluttered feel of the place and may even wonder why you want replacements.

With the house down to essentials, it is bound to look shabby. Decide what can be cleaned or dyed, what sofas and chairs can be remodeled and slipcovered, whether curtains and draperies have had their day. What about fresh paint and wallpaper?

Let your husband help

Now is the time to get your husband into the project. Does your kitchen need modernizing? If you are going to stay here for the long haul, will you eventually need a full bathroom downstairs? Would you both love a fireplace in the room where you spend most of your time?

Does the outside of the house need paint, new roofing, new screens and storms? Would you like more shrubs and plantings, a rock garden, roses? Now that your son is gone, do you need a sit-down mower?

Right now is the time to figure everything you want to do to the house and to determine whether the total investment is practical. If so, work out a plan for doing every-

---

* At the end of the year, you will receive a statement of what your donation brought in cash, which you can list as a contribution on your income tax return. Or you can accept a percentage in cash from your thrift shop, should you prefer to sell on consignment.

thing on your list as soon as possible, paying as you go or with a construction mortgage.*

If your house is in a good neighborhood, a new fireplace, bathroom, paint, and roofing will boost the value of your property, which will be appreciating anyway as prices everywhere go up. You will get back more than you have paid out on the principal of your mortgage, should you decide to sell, and the interest you pay is tax deductible. If you never sell, the improved quality of your everyday life will be worth your investment, and redecorating the house, once it is spruced up inside and out, will be a lot of fun.

If your house is in a deteriorating neighborhood, major repair may not make sense, but strip down to essentials, anyway. Then, groom the lawn, shine the windows, and sparkle up dingy walls inside with paint. Have the carpets, slipcovers, and draperies cleaned, polish the furniture until it glistens, and list your house for sale. (From accompanying my husband, who owns a real estate business, to show houses to prospective buyers, I know that a well-groomed house sells faster than an unkempt one, and new paint in the bathroom and kitchen pushes the price up to cover three times the cost of the job.)

Should your slicked-up house sell immediately, sell your carpeting, draperies, any made-to-order furniture, and as many large pieces as possible to the new owners, taking a big slash under what you once paid, to avoid moving costs. What you can't sell this way and know you will never use again, sell at a garage sale or give to the Salvation Army, taking a tax deduction. Above all, avoid unnecessary moving and storage costs which can be immense.

---

* After talking with workmen, take your remodeling plan and projected costs to your bank, asking for a new mortgage (or an addition to your present mortgage) to cover the total job, but request that money be put into your account as work is done so that you pay interest on construction only as work is completed.

Store only those classic pieces of furniture that you can use anywhere, and move temporarily to a hotel or a clean, comfortable, easy-to-care-for furnished apartment in the same neighborhood. Be grateful for a brief respite from housekeeping and the excuse it gives you for not entertaining at home, and use the hours you used to spend on housework to look for the perfect house or apartment to live in next.

If you know definitely that you will stay in your present town until your husband's retirement and probably afterward, too, before listing your home decide in what neighborhood you want to live next. You may be fortunate to find exactly what you want when your house sells and avoid a double moving expense by shifting to your new home with no intermediate stop. Don't strain for this, however. Far better to sell or donate to charity all of the pieces of furniture you know you will not use again, wherever you live, and rent a small place on a month-to-month basis than to settle for a place you aren't completely sold on.

Don't rush

When you find just what you want, don't rush to move in. By keeping your apartment an extra month, you will save money as well as strain. (When you are uncomfortable, you rush to get things done, make wrong decisions, foolish buys.) Arrange for repairs and necessary painting in your new house before you switch, and shop for furnishings carefully, not skimping on quality and paying particular attention to colors which both you and your husband find compatible.

Money-making intermission

If your husband is to be transferred soon, or for some other reason you know you won't be living in your present town for more than a year or so, invoice your furnishings and sell your house as advised above, but then do not move to an apartment. Look for a good buy on a small, saleable, easy-to-care for home, sure to appreciate.

Before moving from the old house sell all furniture other than the basic pieces that will be useful where you will be living now or later. Then, groom your new little house as you did the other one, and three or four months before moving to your new town, list it for sale. With the mark-up that will come as a result of its good grooming plus natural appreciation, your intermission house should bring in a size-able profit as well as save you rent.

Live well in your little house, but keep your possessions pared way down so that your housework will be minimal, and use every spare minute in this year for self-instruction. Look at what your town has to offer with new eyes. Teach yourself to see!

Absorb impressions for future reference

Visit museums this year, go to art shows, see fashion shows, walk through model rooms in local department stores. Take a flower-arranging course, paint, take instruction in pottery making. Visit nearby historical homes, go to auctions, sign up for tours of old and unusual homes. Visit model homes and apartments, see traveling exhibits of crystal and silver.

At first, you will simply seem to be looking at just so many pictures in frames, so many goblets on a table, so much pottery on a shelf. But eventually you will begin to be aware of the creative mind that conceived each object and you will become conscious of beauty in much around you that you never noticed before. Screened no longer from ideas too big for you, your eyes will see.

"We cannot see things that stare us in the face," said Emerson, "until the mind is ripened; then we behold them, and the time when we saw them not is like a dream."

Now your taste will improve, and you will automatically become more selective. Naturally, the home or apartment you furnish after a year spent in this way will reflect your new awareness. As you make selections now, your new sophistication will delight your husband, enchant your friends, and surprise you. Far from being a year in which you simply marked time, this period of self-improvement will be one that you will never forget.

10

SEVEN POSSIBLE WAYS TO LIVE FROM NOW ON

Now that you are back to two in the family again, there is no need to stay in the neighborhood you once selected for its good schools and playgrounds. Still, you can't take off for just anywhere until your husband's retirement unless you are wealthier than most or he is a pilot or writer, consultant, artist, or other free agent who can name his own home base. The average empty nest husband with ten or fifteen years to go before he can collect from social security, his company pension, and/or annuity has to stay near his work. This limits where you can live, but it doesn't mean that you must stay in the same old neighborhood until your husband is sixty-five. Marking time until retirement is an extravagance no empty nest couple can afford.

While many couples now live twenty-five, thirty, or even more years together after the children leave, the average time an empty nest couple can count on being together is fifteen years. For two persons in their fifties to spend fifteen years planning for a full life after they're sixty-five in

California, Florida, Arizona, or some more comfortable place is a waste of precious years. The time for comfortable living is *now*.

Lots of possibilities

If your husband has fifteen years or less to go until retirement, he fits into one of these categories. Check which one.

1. He is a business or professional man who has lived all his life near where his parents (and probably, yours) once lived, and there is no conceivable business reason for him to transfer to another place at this late date.

2. He is a company man who cannot count on staying put until retirement even though you may prefer this. You will be moving again.

3. Your husband (and perhaps you, too) commutes from a suburb to a large city like New York, Chicago, Cleveland, Atlanta, Los Angeles, or Minneapolis, where you work in advertising, publishing, a stock brokerage house, broadcasting, or some other big-city business that will keep you in a metropolitan area for the next decade even though your husband may not stay with the same agency or company.

4. He works for the government (the post office, maybe) and can either stay put or move to another city or government agency as he chalks up time toward his eventual pension. Or he is a military career man, or he and, maybe, you are professors or teachers.

5. Your husband is a self-starter. As a writer, artist, promoter, land developer, photographer, industrial film maker, or anything else of this nature, he is his own man and can live wherever you both want to live. As far as retiring, he doesn't even know the meaning of the word. He will never retire.

6. He is a farmer. Now that the boys are gone and it is increasingly difficult to make a small farm pay off, there is

no reason for him to knock himself out until he is sixty-five, which (except for a small boost in social security benefits) has nothing to do with when he can retire. Your aim: to get him to sell the farm now and live in ease.

7. Your husband has enough money to do nothing more than what he wants to do from now on. He can travel, invest in a new business, move to a new place. All that is keeping both of you where you are is habit.

To recommend a sure-fire way of life for all empty nesters that will automatically result in a pleasant, custom-made existence after sixty-five would be ridiculous. But here are possibilities available to persons in each of the seven categories.

1. HOMETOWN BOY

Your husband's roots (and probably, yours) go deep in your hometown where you are surrounded by long-time friends, relatives, and probably some of your children and their children. To move far away may be a jolt, but to take a back seat in your town as your children take over can make you old before your time. If the climate is right for you, here are some options.

i) Stay in your same house, spreading out now that the children are gone. Make one of your spare bedrooms into a studio, another, into a den or library or upstairs TV room; or change two bedrooms into a living room-bedroom guest suite complete with pullman kitchen for visiting children and grandchildren from out of town. Prepare for long-time living by putting in a downstairs bath, if there isn't one, and more appliances to make living comfortable. (In case of illness, that upstairs suite can serve as a nurse's quarters.) And then forget age and put that art studio or writing room to good use. Do something now!

ii) Move to a smaller home, all on one floor, near your church and stores and near the green, if you live in a small town. Be sure you're near a motel, where your children and their children can stay when they come from out of town. If you like flowers, get a place with a large lawn and a place for a flower garden and begin now, long before retirement, to make your outdoors a place of beauty. Later, your gardens will be a delight and a hobby. And don't overextend yourself financially. Even though you like your town, get away at least once a year. Such trips call for money, so don't put it all in your home.

iii) If there is an apartment house for over-fifty residents nearby or a settlement for empty nesters like Heritage Village at Southbury, Connecticut, Rossmoor Leisure World at Laguna Hills, California, or Sun City in Arizona, rent or buy a place close to your husband's place of business. Then, until retirement, he can commute to work by car. Such apartments or communities give both him and you a built-in social life and available activities, should you care to take advantage of what's there.

Usually, in places for the over-fifty, you will find a swimming pool, saunas, therapeutic baths, bridge, movies, sewing rooms, art studios, kilns, a good library and—in locations away from the city—golf. Selling your home and investing in a cooperative apartment in a well-planned building or a condominium in a village with a limited number of planned residences makes good sense from a business standpoint. Such units, in all communities we have looked at, appreciate in value every year. With such obvious advantages, why do so many empty nesters hold back? Somehow, they think a move like this is a final commitment, a point of no return. *Not true*. If you don't like your over-fifty environment, you can sell as you would sell any house and move to an apartment or small home right back in the town you came from.

iv) Move to an apartment in a church-owned complex for over-fifty residents. Here you give a "donation" of from $7,500 to $15,000 or more to your church which entitles you to your own quarters for as long as you live at which time your apartment does not go to your heirs, as does a condominium at a retirement village, but to the church, itself, for resale. You get a tax deduction, of course, for your original gift to the church. Call your own church and others in your town for the names of available church-owned residential complexes near you. Usually, you do not have to be a member of the church that owns the complex—but your donation goes there.

If the climate is not right for you where you have lived all your life, do not stick it out just because you are dubious about taking root in a new environment at this late stage. First of all, remember that an empty nest doesn't signify a late stage anymore, and that a man can count on more years after the children leave than his forefathers could count on for life. Think of yourself as being given a bonus life. Then, decide whether you want to live this bonus life in the town and the climate where you have always lived. If so, stay. If not, leave, but obviously you will have some practical considerations to deal with.

As the owner of a small-town business or farm in a northern state, make plans to sell your business or farm and home as many years as possible this side of retirement, but know before you sell where you want to live. If possible, spend several winter vacations in a test situation before actually pulling up stakes.

2. COMPANY MAN

Your community is a business organization, not a town. So far, your husband may have been eastern division manager in one spot, sales manager in another, marketing director in another. (Or, as a career woman, you may work for a chain of stores where you started as a buyer for one store in the Middle West, then a buyer in New York for the whole chain, and now you're manager of a new department store purchased by your company in the South.) You have no roots where you now live, and some day you will be finished with your present affiliation. What are your options?

i) Buy a home where you or your husband grew up, but remember, the same people won't be there anymore, and you have changed. (Besides, there is some reason why you didn't stay put in the first place. Are you sure the old hometown will be more attractive the second time around?) Only if you have children there and/or many friends and love the climate should you think of returning. And even then, don't buy a remote house at the edge of town which promises peace and quiet, unless you have a project coming up that requires peace and quiet. You are geared for activity. Select a home that is made for lots of house guests, plenty of activity, big projects.

ii) Buy a home now where you may eventually retire in a town or vacation spot to which you like to return. This is a good investment because you can rent your vacation house should you be transferred for a time beyond practical traveling distance. But when you are working nearby, you can go there for weekends and vacations. In an ever-changing environment this place can be your home base. Vote there, subscribe to the local paper, become interested in local affairs. Thus, the crossover to your new community when you eventually retire will be an easy one and, at the last minute, should you decide not to settle there, your original investment will have appreciated so you will lose nothing. Then you can have the fun of looking for some place new.

iii) Locate near former business associates, who, like Army career friends, are now almost as close as family. Let's say, one, two, or three couples are buying homes near each other on a favorite Wisconsin lake. Don't say "No" too fast to going there. This could be a great life. Or you and two other couples may form a combine and buy an old farm. (Three couples we know did this in Vermont and are now overseeing the conversion of the old farm house and two barns into three houses. Their three-way involvement makes for efficiency; when one couple can't be in Vermont for several weeks or more, the others take over.) Or maybe you prefer to homestead a plot of land which was part of a government-owned tract. Again, three teachers we know did this ten years ago in California. One who was retired oversaw the building of three adobe houses on three adjoining two-acre plots for which the teachers paid fifty dollars apiece. By now, the three old friends and their wives have retired and live in neighboring houses near others they have come to know, in a warm climate they all appreciate.

iv) Buy a multiple dwelling in a pleasant town or in a resort area, paying for it now as your husband finishes up his working years. Plan eventually to live there and let your rents from apartments, plus your retirement income, support your way of life. Or, if you have a really deep affection for two other couples in your business circle, buy a three-apartment building in the Caribbean or other glamour spot, using your individual apartments as vacation places, eventually retiring there full time. The trips to find what you have in mind will be as much fun as the life you finally work out and, once again, you can rent your apartment when not in use.

Whatever you do, use your remaining time with your company to see the world. Ask for a transfer to a foreign country for a year, take spur trips at your own expense after far-away meetings, store up long vacation allowances for away-from-it-all glamour living.

3. BIG-CITY RESIDENT

After living in a suburb for years for the children's sake, you now have these options.

i) If you and your husband have become involved in community affairs and this town now seems like home, your options are the same as those in the first category on pages 73–75. If, however, you have lived in your town for the past fifteen years just because of its advantages for the children and for the easy commuting, your list of choices is long and varied, as the remaining options illustrate.

ii) If you love museums, the theater, good stores, concerts —all the excitement of a large city—sell your home and move into New York or Chicago or San Francisco or wherever your husband and maybe you go to work, and rent or buy an apartment. If you live in New York and your income is large, here are five secondary options: (a) buy, in addition to your apartment, a weekend country home in Pennsylvania, upper New York State, or Connecticut where you may or may not eventually retire; (b) buy a summer home on Cape Cod, Martha's Vineyard, or Nantucket, Long Island or the Jersey shore where you can fly or drive for weekends and a long summer vacation, and where you may eventually retire; (c) buy a winter place in the Caribbean or in Arizona, South Carolina, Florida, or Mexico, where you can take off for a long winter vacation or occasional long weekends when blizzards come, and, again, where you may or may not eventually retire; (d) rent a year-round vacation place on Long Island or in Pennsylvania, Connecticut, or New Jersey, where you can go for long weekends and for summer and winter vacations; (e) rent a cottage on a lake for a summer vacation, a lodge in Maine for the fall, an apartment in the Caribbean for the winter. Go some place new every time you can get out of town. (Outside of New York, in any other American city, you have similar options—all making for a good and glamorous life.)

iii) If you love converting old houses, you have the same opportunity or more in a city than you have in the country, and you can save money by living in your home as you do your remodeling around you. About twenty years ago, in downtown Chicago, artists, decorators, and other creative people bought dilapidated town houses in the Old Town district, converted them, and now have choice homes in one of the most desirable sections of town. In Boston, friends of ours bought a run-down, three-floor town house for $9,000 near Bunker Hill monument in rough-and-tumble Charlestown, converted this with a little money and lots of imagination, sweat, and love into a showplace now worth at least $60,000 or $70,000. In Philadelphia, others bought a drab house built in 1824 in the old run-down Society Hill section, scheduled for redevelopment with state and federal funds. Today, their elegant home, complete with outdoor garden and swimming pool, is the talk of the town.

Sometimes, you do not have to buy to do a conversion that pays off. In the early 1960s, we rented two apartments in New York City, one above the other, for a total of $375, taking a three-year lease on both with an option to renew at the end of that period for another two years at the same price. Immediately, we changed the two apartments into a duplex, enabling us to have a large living room, kitchen, and forty-foot garden downstairs and two bedrooms and a bath upstairs with a sixteen-foot-square outdoor balcony overlooking the garden. We furnished the duplex from estate auctions in New York, and it was written up in New York papers as a Sixty-first Street dream house. In the meantime, our building was sold to a speculator who wanted to turn a quick profit and couldn't without offering our duplex to prospective buyers. At the end of our three-year lease, he offered us $2,500 *not to renew our available two-year lease*. He made out all right because he sold his building at a third more than he paid for it, and we came out well, too, because our $2,500 profit paid for nearly seven months of our rent. Improving the place where you live in the city is not only an investment in good living, it is often a moneymaker as well; especially if the address of the place where you live is desirable (as was our Sixty-first Street duplex) or the district is due for redevelopment through state or federal funds.

If you are a born-and-bred city person with no craving for trees and grass and birds, stay in your converted city home after retirement and you can go to the opera, the theater, and the museums for the next couple of decades. If that's what you like, enjoy it! And if you want to get away sometimes, sublet your city home furnished. We rented our furnished Sixty-first Street duplex during one of our sojourns in Europe for $800 a month.

iv) If the city is your money pot, and that's all, and you can't wait to get away when your working days are over, enjoy the city now because afterward you will read about plays, the art galleries, the opera, the museums, and be sorry if you failed to take advantage of them. At the same time, be thinking about where you want to live later. Having lived so long in a big city, you may want to live near a large metropolis after you're sixty-five. This, says Del Webb, is one of the reasons for the tremendous success of the retirement community of Sun City, which his corporation has built, twelve miles from fast-growing Phoenix. "Retired people want independence and like owning their own homes in a retirement community where they can make friends. But they also want to be near the action." Look for a place away from the city if you think you will be tired of the bustle at the end of your working years, but be sure that place is near the action. Unless you're a true Thoreau (in which case you wouldn't have worked in the city in the first place) you will want to get back to the city occasionally.

4. GOVERNMENT OR MILITARY MAN

As a government employee in a post office or a federal or state penitentiary, a state employment office, a social service office of some kind, or any of a dozen other bureaus, your husband may have worked in or out of the same town for years. The same holds true of a teacher or a railroad man or anyone else who has chalked up fifteen or twenty or more years toward a retirement pension. Now may be the time for this person to transfer to a possible retirement location. On the other hand, if he is a career man in the army or some other service and has moved and moved, he may want to stay put. Following are options for both types of persons who have the choice of transferring or not transferring to a new location before their earned pension comes due.

i) As empty nesters whose children live far away, you may want to move closer to them and your grandchildren. Instead of waiting until retirement time when your grandchildren will be going away to college, consider transferring now to a new location where your husband can go on in his same line of work. In doing so, however, remember that your children will be busy with their own lives and that you will have to make friends on your own. Still, if you get the location you want and receive full credit toward your pension for your time already served, there is no need to stay behind. Ask for your transfer, and go.

ii) Let's say that you are a government employee's wife, and that starting a business of your own with the help of your husband has been your dream for years. Now that the children are gone, you're ready. Still, you don't want your husband to give up his eventual pension so you hesitate to urge him to quit. Here's the answer: in his spare time and in your full time, get your business going. (A post office employee and his wife in our town run a prosperous catering business. During the day, she calls and makes appointments to handle parties, and he budgets and does bookkeeping when he gets home at night. She shops for food when a party is decided on and does some cooking at home. On the appointed night of a given sit-down dinner or outdoor barbecue, he turns up as a butler or outdoor chef, she becomes the cateress, and they hire a waitress. By the time retirement comes, they will own a profitable business and have his pension, too. Until then, they're making money and having the time of their lives.)

Another government man's wife near us took a beauty course when the children left home, then urged her husband to take his next vacation in Florida where they looked for and found a beauty shop they wanted to buy. He applied for a transfer that came through; they borrowed money for the shop in Florida which they will pay for out of her profits and his salary; last month they moved to the place where they will work and live before and after retirement when he will have his pension. Don't give up your pension if you have only a few years to go, but don't just sit out time, either.

iii) As the wife of a pilot who travels hundreds of thousands of miles a month or of an Army man who is frequently transferred (or of a Red Cross employee or USO worker), you may appreciate the travel opportunities connected with this work, but you have a strong desire for a home base. More than any other type of empty nester, you want *land*. Look for it as you travel, think about it, get it—an old farmhouse, maybe, and acres of land in a country setting you love—and pay for it through the years, holding in your mind the dream of your own Tara, as you go on with your work. Many pilots who have four or five days between trips buy farms in Connecticut or Pennsylvania, near New York airports, or homes on a lake within a hundred miles of the St. Paul-Minneapolis airport, or ranches within that distance of the Los Angeles airport, or orange groves not too far from Miami. Their families have lived on the land while the children have been growing up and going to school, and now that the children have gone, the pilot and his wife have a home base which has increased in beauty and value through the years. Now, free to travel, the wife of the pilot can see the world with him at a discount as he goes on with his work, all of the time knowing the house and the land is waiting for both of them when it comes time to retire.

The military career man has a somewhat different problem. Like former President Eisenhower, who never owned a home until he moved to his Gettysburg farm, an army man wants land of his own; but he makes far less money than a commercial pilot, so he cannot commit himself to as big an investment. At the same time, the expenses of maintaining the members of his family who have traveled with him have been small, so as he goes up in rank he usually has some money to invest. His best bet, if he wants to own land, is to visit the Bureau of Land Management office in any large city in which he finds himself (Anchorage, Alaska; Denver, Colorado; Phoenix, Arizona; etc.) and bid on a tract of land being offered for sale.* Forty-acre tracts in remote sections of Idaho, New Mexico, and Montana, appraised for $500 or $600, can be picked up through a sealed bid for less than $700 or $800. My husband and I have bought this way.

iv) Stay in your same town, if you want to, but urge your husband to do more than walk to that nine-to-five job every day holding out the carrot of his own pension to himself as a pacifier. Suggest he get started in something new that will become a major interest at retirement time. We know a personnel worker in a prison who took a Dale Carnegie course a few years before his retirement and became such an excellent speaker he was in demand at luncheons. He kept on with his regular work until time for retirement, but began assisting at some nighttime Dale Carnegie

* For good land buys, subscribe to the magazine *Our Public Lands,* which lists upcoming sales in all parts of the country. Send $1, subscription price for four issues per year, to Superintendent of Documents, U.S. Government Printing Office, Washington, D.C. 20402.

courses, too. By the time his other work was behind him, he was booked solid for speeches and courses from one week to the next. With a wealth of stories in his background, he is an absolute dynamo on the platform. His wife handles his bookings, travels with him, does publicity in new towns.

The beauty of any job that keeps a man and woman on the move and pays an eventual pension is that through the years it enables them to consider many possible places to live. The trick is to decide where to retire long before the settled-for time. Begin thinking about this seriously the day your last child leaves home.

5. THE SELF-STARTER

The self-motivated man is a free soul, and you are lucky to be married to one because you can live anywhere. Never one to hang on to a job or a situation out of fear, the husband can pick up almost any time and go anywhere. With such a man, the wife's options are legion.

i) All you have to ask is "Where do we want to live?"— On an island in the sun, on a houseboat, in a converted stone fortress, on a mountaintop, on a ship at sea? You name it, you can have it. You may have stayed in one community while the children have been growing up, but there is no need for that now. Right now, write down where you want to live. Then talk to your husband and get ready. Because once he approves of your plan, that's where you can be.

ii) If you and your husband are photographers, you can put your trade to use anywhere. A Connecticut photographer friend who loves to travel owns a condominium at Heritage Village, the owners of which built a darkroom for him when he bought it. They also sublet his furnished duplex for him when he and his wife take off on a trip. Several times a year, he goes on a cruise, giving slide

lectures about the islands at which the ship will be stopping. At another time, he may make an industrial film on
assignment for a company like General Motors or Pepsi-
Cola. His tool is his camera; his corporation is in his
head. Another photographer friend of ours moved to St.
Croix and set up an inn where he entertains art directors
from New York coming down to do jobs for agencies. The
inn paid off so well he bought a wharf with a warehouse
building that he turned into cooperative apartments which
he sold one by one. Soon he was in real estate and now is
immensely successful. But still he doesn't stay put. Interviewed recently as one of the most successful men in the
Caribbean, living a life to be envied by all, he said with a
shake of his head, "But there comes a moment when I've got
to take off, get away, go to some place new." This man has a
creative mind and can live anywhere. With his knowledge
now of both photography and real estate development, he
has two tools to work with—and if he ever got in a spot
where he wanted something that neither tool could help
him to achieve, obviously he'd find another.

iii) As an artist or a writer, your husband needs a place
to work away from people—still, he may want stimulation
when not at the drawing board or typewriter. Also, he has
to be close enough to a large city to peddle his wares unless he is so well established that the world comes to him.
His only danger is that he may take an allied job (copy-
writer or art director in an agency, editor or art director
for a magazine, or advertising manager for a printing company) that he doesn't care about which could be as frustrat-
ing to him as waiting out a pension is to an interviewer in
a state employment office. Once again, when the children
were in school, he may have hesitated to take the plunge—
but, now, encourage him to go ahead. Suggest that he get a
teaching job in a college or university, which will leave
him time to paint or write away from the classroom. Or

take whatever money you have and buy an old house or barn far from a city and urge him to use his creative talent to help you do over the house while continuing to paint or write, too. (If he has artistic talent, the house will appreciate in value as you improve it. If he gets joy out of doing over old places, sell the first house and convert another, adding to your income this way until his painting, writing or whatever else he does brings in enough for good living. Otherwise, live in the house you do over and keep on doing what you like to do.) Your first consideration: do the work you were cut out to do, no matter what. Let your environment work itself out around you.

iv) As a buyer and seller of land, your husband is as free as the writer who can write anywhere. His sixth sense tells him what island is due to become popular, what cities are due to be troubled next summer and in what direction families will be moving when the trouble comes, and how to publicize the location of land that he owns. He also knows how to shop for the money the way others shop for groceries, how to buy for little and sell for more. With this in his kit, he can live anywhere and do well. Hopefully, you can appreciate his talent and move as he moves. (When the children were growing up and you wanted roots, you may have found the uncertainty of life a little rough.) A lot more women should be so lucky!

6. THE FARMER

The fact that you and your husband may be alone on the farm now that the children are gone may be a blessing in disguise. Far from being romantic about the old place, you have really had it. With the cost of equipment going up and no help to be had, your husband is pushing himself from morning to night, and you know he should slow down. So what are your options?

i) You can sell the farm to a large-scale absentee land-owner who will hire a manager to do the actual farming. Then buy a small house in a nearby town where you have been going to church for years and know the storekeepers and have friends.

ii) You can take what capital you have and make a small payment on a house and rent the farm, taking a percentage of the proceeds. (The rent you receive will pay your mortgage payments.) With more time, your husband can work with the extension division of your state agricultural college and local conservation commission to get help on what-to-grow-when, on soil analysis, on how to use the land to best advantage, on what federal funds are available. With more time for head work, he may find that overseeing the work of others will bring in more than doing the farming himself. In the meantime, you will be living with far less strain.

iii) Urge your husband to put your problem up to your children who may want you to hold on to the farm, knowing that it is bound to appreciate in value. Make a deal with them. Tell them you will keep the farm, rent the house to someone in a nearby town who wants to keep his children in the country, and rent the land to the farmer whose land adjoins yours. And someday it will still be theirs if they want it. But, in the meantime, they have to give you the money you need for a home someplace else, which will appreciate in value and which you will also will to them. Then, take off for a town like Sun City in Arizona or to Leisure World in Laguna Hills, California, where many from your state may be in residence. Buy a home (for from $18,000 to up to just about anything you want to pay) and start fresh in an adult community with others who are also glad to make friends. Don't worry that your children and friends won't come to see you; you will be swamped with calls from vacationers who can stay at a nearby inn.

iv) You can remain on the farm, if you like, but change the emphasis. Maybe you can turn the old house into a nursing home or build cottages on the farm for summer vacationers or sell your property to a real estate developer for a country club and golf course, where you can stay on as caretakers.

v) You can stay on the farm during the working months but get away in the winter. At Castle Hot Springs resort near Wickenburg, Arizona, we met a farmer and his wife from Nebraska who work hard at home until January 15, then leave to work at the resort until March 15, he as a gardener, she as a desk clerk. "It's ideal for us," they told us.

7. RICH MAN

Nobody's heart bleeds for your husband and you. You can maintain a winter and summer home if you like, or live full time on a boat, or travel anywhere that suits your fancy, or meet your friends at any resorts you and they find appealing. Furthermore, even though we hear on all sides about the shortage of domestic help, it can be found. But you will not find full happiness unless you become involved in something. Here are things to do about it:

i) Buy a business and make it grow just for the fun of it. Maybe you will stay at a resort hotel sometime that is up for sale. You can see on the spot how it can be improved. Buy it and make it pay. Your vacations there will be ten times as enjoyable because you will be involved. Or, if you don't want to get into the actual running of a business, help a young couple you believe in buy a resort. Vacation there occasionally. Watch it take off.

ii) Get involved in conserving the beauty of the place where you live. Work with state, federal, and county conservation people to maintain the beauty of your community, prevent pollution, prohibit gravel pits, preserve open spaces. Get acquainted with zoning laws, talk to your state conservation office about the specific needs of your particular town, talk to men's and women's clubs about what can be done by organizations and individuals.

iii) When you travel, don't go to the same old places, even though you are comfortable there and know all the help and the visitors. Stay at new places, see new people, travel new ways. And, in return, invite new people to your home. Your interests will broaden.

In this chapter, you have read a dozen suggestions for bridging the time between child rearing and retirement with a plan for the future that is bound to expand your daily life with every step you take. Read the suggestions that appeal to you aloud to your husband. With his help, work out the alternative ways of life that can make sense for you. As you read this book, one of these plans will become more and more appealing. You will be on your way.

"Try on" a variety of lives

Hopefully, you will return to this chapter as you go on thinking about where you eventually want to live. Read all the suggestions, not just those specifically for people who are doing what you are doing. One of the thoughts for another may spark you to go in a new direction. This, rather than to give you an actual blueprint for your future, is the purpose of this book.

As you come close to a commitment, find a way to "try on" the life you are considering. If you have always dreamed of living in Europe, try subletting your home and then rent a house for the summer in a village on the Mediterranean or elsewhere before you actually pull up stakes and take off for good. Do the same for a few months before selling your home in a suburb and buying a cooperative apartment to be close to the action in the city. Rent your home to others, and sublet an apartment in the section of the city you have in mind.

We keep a furnished apartment at Sutton Place and Fifty-fifth Street in New York City. Twice in a ten-year period we have sublet this apartment for a year to empty nesters who wanted to "try on" city life before deciding on their future plans. At the end of one couple's lease, our renters couldn't wait to sell their home in Naugatuck and move to Manhattan, which they found was really right for them. The other couple couldn't get back to Bayside fast enough. The only way to find out what you want is to try it. But to make a permanent commitment before you are really sure where you want to live is silly, especially when there are so many easy ways to decide whether the course you are considering is right for you.

11

TAKE JUST ONE STEP

As you put your front foot down for one step in life, your back foot is already coming up to take the next step. Headed in the right direction, progression becomes automatic.

If you have begun the simple health program suggested in Part One, one new step is now following another almost without your noticing. Each day, as you continue to cut down on fat-makers and eat your custom-made vitality boosters, you will become more and more aware of a change in your physical tone. Along with this, you will notice a new ability to get things done because your stepped-up energy simply won't let you be passive.

Soon, your entire life will begin to reflect a woman with a far happier and more adventurous disposition. As your life-style changes, your home will begin to change, too. Then, anything "old hat" won't do.

In doing over a house, follow the basic procedure recommended for redoing your body: take one step at a time. First step, invoice; second step, pare down; third step, spruce up. First, a look; then, a thought; then, action.

All this without big money

Refurbishing your home can cost as little proportionately as redoing you. (If you have shopped now for energy-producing foods, you can see already that your grocery bills will be going down, not up, and certainly getting outdoors everyday will cost you nothing.) Getting rid of unattractive space-crammers in your rooms and closets is no more extravagant than throwing out half-used packages and bottles of old food in your refrigerator; and taking a good straight look at the furniture in your home is free.

Doing away with furniture you are tired of can actually bring in money; and brightening up your home inside and out adds to its value whether you move now or later. Take your choice of selling or renting your home while you work out a better way of life; either will put dollars into your bank account. So don't tell yourself that you can't make a change in the way you live for lack of cash.

As you select new furnishings, you will probably pay more per item, but you will be buying quality classics from now on that won't get shabby, won't fall apart, and you won't get tired of. So, even here, your total annual expenditure does not have to be more than now. Think about this the next time you see a woman of your age who looks and lives with elegance. Turn off any temptation to excuse yourself with, "Sure, I could live and look like that, too, if money were no object." With no more money coming in than now, you can look and live better than you ever imagined.

Don't try to do everything at once

Don't throw up your hands and groan when you think about what it would mean to clear out the old house and move to a new place. For the time being, don't even think about moving. Simply clear out one room or closet or drawer. This will help you to see repairs that should be made, things to be discarded, replacements that are needed. Follow through and you will be on your way. By taking one step at a time, you eventually can work out a way of life far more glamorous than anything you can possibly anticipate from where you sit today.

More about our duplex—or
"How one step started us toward the life we love"

When my husband and I rented two one-above-the-other New York apartments in the early sixties and changed them into a duplex, we had no idea we were taking a step that was to change our entire lives. We had recently married, and because we had a total of six his-and-her children who would be coming with their mates to visit from time to time, we had to have larger quarters than either of the two apartments we had leased and lived in as single empty nesters. Our solution: to sublet both of our premarriage apartments furnished and take a larger place that we could furnish from scratch. This was the step that changed our world.

At the time, my husband was a commercial artist and, I know now, a "born architect," and I was a vice-president in an advertising agency and, I know now, a "born hand-raiser at auctions." Once given the creative opportunity to change six drab back rooms into a dreamboat duplex, we tackled our project with pent-up fervor which amazed our practical friends who couldn't see putting that kind of effort into city property that did not belong to us and never would. After years of regimented New York living, we were having the time of our lives.

Within a couple of months, we had a great kitchen and dining area downstairs with walls lined with French windows opening out onto a forty-foot garden, a powder room, and a dream of a living room (with a wood-burning fireplace) with huge French doors also opening to the garden. Leading to the upstairs was a small circular stairway, which my husband painted dull gold. On the second floor we had a large master bedroom opening out on a sixteen-foot-square deck, a large bath, a large book-lined study (which could be converted to a bedroom), and a huge closet that we made by utilizing space left over from the upstairs kitchen.

About the time we moved in, the Sulgrave Hotel near us on Park Avenue came down, and its contents were offered at auction. In one day we bought carpets for upstairs and down, transparent gold draperies for our living room, lined hand-printed draperies for all our other windows, a bed and handsome satinwood chest for our bedroom, chaises for our upstairs terrace, exquisite chairs and tables, and a custom-made hide-a-bed sofa for our living room, plus wrought-iron chairs and tables and umbrellas from the hotel's garden for our garden. For all our purchases we paid no more than we had paid in our former apartments for the living room furniture alone. Buying at the Sulgrave really opened our eyes.

Now we knew that furniture need not be new to be beautiful and that buying at an auction is a marvelous way to get real bargains. After that, we went to an estate auction on Saturday instead of to a Broadway matinee. I was hooked, but it didn't matter, because time after time we came home with elegant pieces of furniture and wall decorations that made our duplex a showplace.

During our second year in the duplex, we were sent to Europe on a special assignment, so we sublet the Sixty-first Street place (as well as our two original apartments) at a profit of several hundred dollars a month. Once again we learned something of importance. Many New Yorkers will pay far more for a furnished place than they would have to pay for the same space and the individual pieces of furniture if they started on their own from scratch. There was a business here.

When we returned from Europe, our landlord offered us the $2,500 to give up our lease. Just about then, my husband's lease on his former apartment was also coming to an end, so we decided to live temporarily in my old apartment and take the furniture from the duplex and from his apartment to the country where we hoped to find a small weekend place. Through a fluke, we heard about the auction of a farm in New Milford, Connecticut, and attended. There, in a lush out-of-the-way valley, we bid on a house, barn, and fifty acres, just as we had bid at New York estate auctions on mirrors, paintings, china, and lamps. In ten minutes and for $18,000 we bought a boulder-strewn farm, tangled with laurel and dogwood and white birch on a hilly piece of land equal to the size of half a hundred football fields.

"Someday we will live here full time," we said to each other, and then we looked around. Maybe that day would be soon. The weathered silver-gray chestnut barn could be a marvelous two-floor home for weekenders; the trapper's cabin up by the deer blind could be a hideaway bungalow for nature lovers; the swamp could eventually be a lake, and beside it could go a glass-fronted home for summer people. Meanwhile we could live in the house which we could expand one room at a time as our projects grew.

We put the furniture from the duplex and Cle's old Manhattan apartment into the square white house, which in those days had no running water, no furnace, and no bathroom, but was immaculate and sound and had a great wood range for cooking and heat. (It did have electricity.) Weekends for the first six months, we drove up from New York and lived in the old house as my husband oversaw conversion of the barn which changed before our eyes into a handsome two-floor electric home with great exposed beams and walls of rare chestnut inside and out.

By this time we had figured out a way to work full time in the country, so we sublet our one remaining apartment in New York and moved into our barn. Immediately, we began digging the lake and doing over the house. Within another year it was all finished.

Now it is seven years, seven books, many advertising assignments, and three houses later. We still sublet the New York apartment with the furniture that was in it long ago, rent the barn furnished year-round to weekenders from Manhattan, rent the hilltop cabin furnished to a nature-loving lawyer from Hartford, rent the vacation house near the lake to a New York doctor and his family.

Our house, which rambles all over the side of the hill, now has four baths and three kitchens and an office at one end where my husband conducts a real estate business when he's not doing art assignments. Both of us find it difficult to remember that we ever lived any other way.

To work out a way of life that is as right for you as our life in the country is for us, we have one suggestion: *Begin with a single step*. The next steps will follow of their own accord as your direction becomes clear. And, you can take it from two who have tried it, they will lead you to a way of life that at this moment even you cannot believe.

PART THREE

NOW A NEVER-ENDING SUPPLY OF DOLLARS FOR WHATEVER YOU WANT

12

RICHER THAN YOU KNOW

Marketing people say that the woman in an empty nest has "the most awesome purchasing power in the history of America." You may not think of yourself as wealthy, but here are their reasons for thinking so.

1. If your husband is like most men in an empty nest, he is at the peak of his earning power.
2. Your household expenses are down now that the children are gone.
3. The big bite that has been coming out of your family income for education is now yours again. (This is the same as a raise.)
4. Your home is probably paid for.*
5. You can earn extra money on your own.†
6. Any inherited money coming in arrives about now.
7. You know quality, so you are hard to fool. And by this time you want and know where to find the best.

For one of several reasons (care of an older family member, inability of a husband to work, uninsured hospital bills, college bills you have agreed to pay back, lingering dependency of one of the children, etc.) your financial state may

---

* Sixty-nine percent of today's empty nesters own their own homes.
† Fifty percent of all women between forty-four and fifty-five are in the labor force, more than in any other age group.

not be the best, but unless hard luck has really rapped, you have never had it this good. The trick is to invest wisely for an easy long-term retirement as you do what you want to do now. You have done your stint in an unsteady world. From now on, you deserve to live well.

Luckier than the very rich

Because you can remember exquisitely happy times in a home far more modest than the one you can now afford, you are more fortunate in one important way than those with great wealth. You won't keep looking for happiness elsewhere.

"The rich," Charlotte Curtis, women's news editor of *The New York Times,* was quoted as saying in a recent article in *Look,* "search for a vacation to get away from a vacation. They leave Mexico to go to Sardinia because they're exhausted. They leave Sardinia to go to Paris because they're exhausted. And so on. . . ." And *Look*'s senior editor, Frank Trippett, added: "You may find fun elsewhere—but only the fun you bring with you. For that is where it's at."

As we have noted, your inner and outer comfort depends on specific physical and psychological needs which remain unchanged whether you are at home or far away. This does not require that you be homebound, but it does mean that you should know what factors in your environment make for satisfaction or dissatisfaction and to find the first and avoid the second wherever you go.

While a great deal of money may not be essential to your comfort, the more dollars you have (up to a point), the more convenient it will be for you to work out a satisfactory environment wherever you find yourself. Therefore, if you don't have all the money you need to live the way you want to live, you can find a way to get more. Specific suggestions are in the next chapter.

13

NINE OPPORTUNITIES YOU NEVER HAD BEFORE

You have three money-producing tools today that you didn't have to the same degree when the children were small:

1. Time—Now that the children are gone, you can put to use in a new way the hours you used to spend with them.
2. Competence—After years of running a home, you have a built-in management viewpoint which any employer or business partner will appreciate.
3. Money—Through careful investing, your added dollars can beget dollars.

Additional income will come from your putting these tools to work in one or more of these areas:

1. Helping your husband with what he wants to do.
2. Earning money yourself.
3. Wise investments.

You may never have worked a day in your life. Forget this and decide what you would like to do if you could begin a new career tomorrow.

"Each mind has its own method," wrote Emerson. On the

next page, check the money-earning avenue that is most appealing to you. As you read further, you will find specific suggestions for a four-step plan that will help you achieve what you want. Later, write down: (1) where to get additional training; (2) where you can learn on the job; (3) where to find needed capital; (4) exactly where you eventually want to be. With these facts in front of you, you can go ahead.

Check the most appealing career

WORKING WITH YOUR HUSBAND

1. Become your husband's secretary, salesgirl, assistant, or bookkeeper, saving on outgo and helping to build up his business from the inside.
2. Make a place for yourself through an expansion of his business. (Examples: add a foreign boutique to his department store; get into ready-to-wear, if he's a fabric manufacturer; put a gift shop in his restaurant, etc.)
3. Become his business manager. Study his profit and loss sheets, find new efficiency methods, study tax laws, investigate diversification possibilities, etc.

WORKING ON YOUR OWN

1. Take a brush-up course at an employment office, business school, or college and do what you started to do long ago.
2. Do something creative (writing, pottery-making, photography, etc.) which you know you have a talent for.
3. Run your own business (restaurant, beauty shop,

ad agency, radio station, riding stable, day-care center, etc.).

MAKING MONEY WITH MONEY

1. Invest in stocks. Take an adult education course in investments and a correspondence course through the New York Stock Exchange.* Also, as a start, form a stock-buying club with a group of friends. Later, as you gain more knowledge, you can go ahead on your own.
2. Invest in real estate. Take an adult education course in real estate; then, make a study of land values in and around home. Buy a large tract when possible; sell in pieces.
3. Buy old houses and fix up to either rent or sell.†

Later in the book you will find where to go to school and/or get a part-time job to help you get started in the work you want.

---

* Get a job as a receptionist in a brokerage firm. Learn stock-buying principles through a correspondence course for employees who want to be brokers.
† Rent furnished rather than unfurnished for better depreciation on your income-tax return.

14

A FOOLPROOF SYSTEM THAT MULTIPLIES DOLLARS AS YOU SPEND

If you get the figures together for your annual income tax, you will have no trouble filling in the chart on pages 106–107, which tells at a glance how much of your income is going for investments each year and what is simply blown. If your husband is the money handler, encourage him to help you to fill in the blanks by referring to your last year's income tax return and to explain anything you don't understand. With your complete financial picture always at hand, you won't be confused in an emergency and will be able to help your husband with his long-term plans for retirement, whether you work or not.

A potful of money

"All any empty nest couple has to do to live as well in retirement as before," says Don French, member of the President's Club of the Connecticut General Life Insurance

Company, "is to divide all the money that comes into the house into two pots: 75 percent for the spend-it pot,* 25 percent for the save-it-pot, which earns as you earn."

A tall order—to save 25 percent of your income? It can be done through investments in four areas: social security and business investments; insurance; your home and other real estate; and personal property, like furnishings, jewelry, and art. Chances are you're putting away pretty close to that now. Fill in the figures and you will find you're richer than you know.

* For your peace of mind, you will naturally want to be solvent. But beyond paying on time for your regular living expenses, the way you spend the rest of this 75 percent is up to you.

PERSONAL SAVINGS-SPENDING CHART
FOR ONE YEAR ONLY

Total amount of income after taxes last year (unless this year was exceptionally good or bad, in which case take an average one) for one or both partners   _____

Did you put away one fourth of this amount through savings in four categories? Fill in blanks and find out.

1. AMOUNT SAVED IN CONNECTION WITH BUSINESS
   a. Social Security
      (Amount paid out last year by one or both partners)   _____
   b. Ownership in a business
      (Amount paid into business last year toward ownership or improvements)   _____
   c. Pension and/or profit-sharing plan
      (Amount paid by you and/or your company last year)   _____

   TOTAL SAVED THROUGH BUSINESS INVESTING   _____

2. AMOUNT SAVED IN INSURANCE
   a. Permanent life insurance
      (Total premiums paid out for permanent life insurance, not term, building up a cash value)   _____
   b. Total premiums paid for annuities   _____
   c. Repayment of insurance loan   _____

   TOTAL SAVED IN INSURANCE   _____

3. AMOUNT SAVED IN REAL ESTATE
   a. Equity in your home
      (Total paid last year on your mortgage, minus interest)   _____
   b. Total paid out for home improvements (like bathroom, fireplace, landscaping) designed to increase value of home   _____
   c. Equity in second home or cottage
      (How much did you pay on principal?)   _____
   d. Other real estate
      (Did you buy land for resale or invest in income-producing property? How much went last year toward the principal?)   _____

   TOTAL SAVED IN REAL ESTATE   _____

4. AMOUNT SAVED IN PERSONAL
   PROPERTY
   a. Stocks—including mutual funds   _____
      (Subtract the stocks you sold and
      broker's commission from what
      you paid out for new stocks.)
   b. Bonds   _____
      (Figure as you did above for
      stocks.)
   c. A savings account   _____
      (What did you actually bank?)
   d. Personal effects   _____
      (What did you spend for dia-
      monds, paintings, rare book col-
      lection, or any other purchase
      bound to hold its own or increase
      in value? Do not count clothing,
      automobile, furniture, etc., which
      will diminish in value.)

   TOTAL SAVED IN PERSONAL   _____
   EFFECTS

To figure what you saved last year in comparison to what you took in, total what you saved in four categories of saving. Then, divide this total into your total income (figure at top of chart). Now you know what you saved in comparison to what you paid out. More than 25 percent saved to 75 percent spent? Keep this up and you will have nothing to worry about ever. Less than 25 percent saved? You have some thinking to do.

More money to invest

If you are putting no more than 10 or 15 percent of your income after taxes into your save-it pot, here are painless ways to boost this to 25 percent.

1. Buy a home instead of renting. The amount you pay on your principal counts as saving, and your interest is tax deductible so leaves more after taxes. Buy wisely, in this time of increased demand, and your house will appreciate.

2. Once the children leave, change your long-term life insurance protection plan or annuity to a paid-up

policy with a cash value that will appreciate. Invest what you paid in premiums in a variable annuity (designed to bring in a fluctuating but increasing income), or a parcel of land, or a multiple dwelling.

3. Invest found money in income-producing bonds by reducing expenditures in five areas: food and liquor (buy store brands instead of national food brands; serve wine with dinner rather than cocktails before); transportation (drive a small non-gas-eating car without lots of gadgets; take advantage of family or excursion rates when traveling); clothing and personal needs (buy classics you don't get tired of; learn to sew; buy drugs, vitamins, etc. at a discount store); vacations (rent a place with several others, taking your turn, or buy a second home, renting when not in use); gifts (buy at sales through the year for year-round giving or give a community gift, such as an old schoolhouse to your children that can be fixed up as a lodge).

4. Add to the family income by going to work yourself.

5. Ask yourself before you plan a large party, an expensive trip, or a big new purchase, whether you are going to get back value received for what you're putting out. Cut out meaningless spending.

Once you accept the logic of the 25 to 75 percent savings-spending plan, you will enjoy making it work. And, certainly, you will appreciate the long-time security it is bound to bring.

15

TEN SURE-FIRE WAYS
TO BUILD A BIGGER
NEST EGG

This is the time when you and your husband are most apt to inherit money. How you handle these bonus dollars along with any surplus left over from your husband's regular income and/or yours will determine your eventual worth and what you will have to live on from now on.

Some women, with a good head for figures, like the game of making money. Such women can handle their own money as well as any business manager and can be of far more help to a husband as a financial partner or investment scout than by working for a paycheck from an outsider. If you have such a bent (and if your husband gets a kick out of your helping him to make his and your money grow) here are ten sure-fire ways to multiply dollars.

Ten ways to build a bigger nest egg

What to do	How to do it	Why?
1. Scout around the outskirts of a large city for an old farm just beyond where land has tripled in the last few years. Buy and hold for at least five years.	Let land sit or rent it to a neighboring farmer which gives you a depreciation allowance against your current income. Eventually sell land on installment sales plan.	Boom land goes up faster than other commodities and compensates in inflation period for weakened dollar. Selling off section by section over a period of years cuts down capital-gains profit subject to income tax in given year.
2. Search for predeveloped land where swelling population and diminishing open spaces are pushing up values. Buy a large tract, hold for six months, sell in small parcels.	Combine funds with other investors; pay 20 percent to 25 percent down; include tax deductible prepaid interest in down payment.	In the first year, you can get back total investment through small parcel sales; also, deductible interest, and spread sales cut taxes on capital gains profit.
3. Buy a quaint old house, railroad station, or school house, and remodel. Use for home or weekend or vacation place while remodeling; rent furnished when finished; sell later.	Get construction mortgage figured on total amount needed for purchase and repair. Take money in three installments as work is done. (Bank examiner will inspect work before paying; you pay interest from time to time when money comes.)	Quaint old homes are in demand, both by renters and buyers. Rent furnished and you get a good spreadout tax depreciation. Doing over house will be fun, and selling will be easy.
4. As a self-employed doctor, dentist, farmer, writer, painter, store owner, accountant, either your husband or you can set up a tax deductible retirement plan under the Keogh Act.	You can set aside up to $2,500 a year from your income with tax deferred until you retire, which can be at sixty-five or later.	Self-employed individuals can now build a tax deductible retirement plan similar to plans offered by large corporations. Talk to your tax advisor.

What to do	How to do it	Why?
5. Invest in income property.	Buy a well-constructed duplex or apartment house (or buy an old wharf, government building, or giant barn that you can convert to apartments or condominiums with help of construction mortgage).	While the federal ruling calls for a minimum of 80 percent payment on stock, you can buy income property for 20 percent down. Rents and/or condominium sales pay for investment, and if you live in one unit your housing will be taken care of as property appreciates.
6. Buy a small business with a promising future (e.g., kennel, village store, antique shop, art gallery, inn, fancy candy shop, cheese place, liquor store, fisherman's shack, sports shop, gift shop, dress shop).	Buy where your husband eventually wants to retire. Get business going (with help of paid helper) during your husband's vacations and over weekends. Then, you stay on premises (or at least on call) and let him come weekends until he can cross over and you can work together full time.	Somebody has paid your husband thousands of dollars for what he knows. Now, if he wants to, he can put this know-how to work for himself with the help of the government. (SCORE, Management Division, Washington, D.C., gives professional help at no cost to small businesses in eight hundred communities. Write there.)
7. Suggest that your husband (and you as his assistant) become consultants.	Mail out twenty-five letters to businessmen your husband absolutely knows he can help to make money. Figure his per diem; charge on the basis of his per diem earnings in his last job and extra for you. All you need is one contract to get going.	Business needs what your husband knows if he is a retired army engineer, navy officer, cattleman, horse buyer, ad man, research expert, travel authority, or good at his work in any area. (Before writing to a given business, put down their needs on one side of the paper; what your husband and you can offer on the other; then, go.)

111

What to do	How to do it	Why?
		A regular annuity provides a fixed income. Noting that stock prices went up seven times as fast as living costs for several inflationary years, experts believe stock is a better hedge against inflation than an annuity.
8. Study the stock market, paying particular attention to mutual funds; invest in a fund with stocks in corporations that are growing faster than average.	Before your husband's retirement, invest in a growth fund; afterward, in an income-producing fund with secondary emphasis on growth.	
9. Suggest to your husband that you talk to an insurance company about a variable annuity.	Ask your insurance man for full details about a variable annuity designed to help you cope before and after retirement with rising costs.	With a variable annuity your dollars are invested in a common stock rather than in fixed interest-bearing investments such as bonds. So your monthly income varies depending on the performances of investments. Therefore, the more you invest during high-income-producing years, the more income you will have after retirement if stocks go up.
10. Set up a living trust.	Talk to an estate planner about helping you to set up a trust, which, in effect, becomes an individual tax payer on its own, thus saving you much in taxes.	The cost of setting up a trust is nominal; the savings on taxes and to ycur estate is great.

Not a big-time operator

Not every woman is Hetty Green. You may be completely disinterested in money, or actually find the thought of any money operation more complicated than a grocery allowance slightly distasteful. Fine, let your husband handle all finances. But for your own protection, ask him to sit down with you some night and explain just what you can expect in the future if anything happens to him. Many widows are surprised to have less to live on than they thought they would have, and many are disorganized, frightened, and lost. Do pay attention to your husband's records and don't turn an inheritance that comes to you over to him without taking note of where the money goes. No matter how good a business-man he is, you should want to know where your money is going and understand why it is being spent there. As you become involved, you may find out that you have more talent for the money game than you realized. Who knows? You may even find that wheeling and dealing is fun.

16

EVERYDAY ELEGANCE WITH OR WITHOUT A FORTUNE

You don't have to have a lot of money to live comfortably, but you do have to have enough. Without what you need to live the way you like to live, you are going to be concerned, and, as Somerset Maugham said, "There is nothing so degrading as the constant anxiety about one's means of livelihood." Once you feel secure, your ability to live elegantly has nothing to do with what you have stashed away in the bank. Far more important than cash are these five factors.

1. Your lack of need to prove anything with the way you live.
2. Daily maintenance.
3. Taste.
4. Good manners.
5. The desire to keep on learning.

Insistence on quality

If you have appraised your finances as advised, you know how you can afford to live. Later, your fortune may sky-rocket, but don't stretch now to prove to others you can live on a grand scale. But don't skimp, either. Live with fewer possessions, if you must, but insist on quality. This is the master key to elegance.

Daily maintenance

Far better to have a small, exquisitely cared-for home than a large one that is going to seed. The same holds true for wardrobe, automobile, flower gardens, everything. When you begin to let things go, elegance goes, too. Make maintenance a rule.

Taste

Your taste determines your choice of clothes, furnishings, jewelry, magazines, friends, even the words you use. If you have innate good taste, you are lucky. If in doubt, seek the advice of an expert, and learn, learn, learn.

Good manners

Life is easier for the courteous than for the pushers. To be truly courteous, strive for tolerance, "grace under pressure," and the courage to be yourself as well as to master everyday rules of etiquette. "Bravery," said Thackeray, "never goes out of fashion." Strive for the bravery to be you, and you will accept others for what they are. This is courtesy.

Love of life

"How I long for a little ordinary enthusiasm," said Jimmy Porter in *Look Back in Anger*. "Just enthusiasm, that's all. I want to hear a warm, thrilling voice cry out, 'Hallelujah! Hallelujah! I'm alive!' " Acquire this enthusiasm for life, and you will automatically learn more about everything. As this interest comes, growth takes place, and your environment will reflect this growth.

Final result—everyday elegance

When your daily life reflects your inner elegance, you will spend less because you will have no need to prove anything to anyone. You will lead the good life automatically, and no matter how much money you do or do not have you can forget the Joneses forever. They will be keeping up with you.

PART FOUR

HOW TO USE
THE GOD-GIVEN
TALENT THAT IS
YOURS ALONE

17

WHAT DO YOU DO EASILY THAT OTHERS FIND DIFFICULT?

"Doing easily what others find difficult is talent," Henri Amiel wrote a hundred years ago. "Doing what is impossible for talent is genius."

If you are a genius, you are producing something of quality as naturally as an oyster produces a pearl (which is a comparison once made by Truman Capote), and your work is your life. Yet, if your aptitude falls just this side of genius, you may not even know that you are gifted. You do the unusual so easily that you can't believe everyone can't do the same. This chapter will change this attitude forever.

What did you like to do as a child?

Were you a good ice skater in school, tops at tennis, good at golf? If you do not swim, play tennis, or golf today, you are denying yourself pleasure related to your inner rhythm.

Did you like to read as a child, daydream a lot, enjoy

movies and plays? You have the mind of a storyteller. Did you like to draw or paint? Were you a good musician? Did you excel in manual training, in cooking, in sewing? You should be doing this now.

Did you like to sell things? Was making money fun? Were you a whiz at math, or were languages your favorite subject? What about history?

Did you really enjoy camp? Like to farm? And garden? What about animals? And little children? And birds?

Think back. Did you really like to go to school? Enjoy digging into a subject until you knew all there was to know about it? Write down the activity that gave you the most pleasure in your early years.

What did you want to be?

As you got older, did you want to be a tennis pro, a writer, or an artist? A jazz pianist or dress designer or a restaurateur? A doctor or a nurse or a teacher? A diplomat, a business tycoon or the first woman governor of your state? Write *that* down.

Look for the connection

Think about the relationship between what you enjoyed as a child and what you wanted to be later on. If you loved school, you wanted to be a teacher; if you loved selling things, you wanted a business of your own; if you loved speaking pieces, you dreamed of being an actress. How close have you come? Write down now what activity outside of raising your children has given you satisfaction as an adult. (Examples: training dogs, teaching kindergarten, going into politics, dancing, playing in a band, etc.)

Next step

The greater the relationship between the three you wrote down, the easier it will be for you to find your next step.

If what you have done in the last twenty-five years has had nothing to do with what you wanted to do, it is not too late today. You have a vein of talent that should be mined.

Take this simple test

In the left-hand column on page 122 write down ten activities that you dislike doing. (Examples: iron clothes, work in a garden, jog, play any kind of game, take care of children, or anything else you don't care for.) In the right-hand column, write down ten things you like to do or would like to do if you had the opportunity. (Examples: dance, play bridge, cook gourmet dinners, take photographs for money, drive a car, paint, go back to college, run a small retail business. Or any of a hundred other activities.)

Ten things I dislike doing	Ten things I like to do
1.	1.
2.	2.
3.	3.
4.	4.
5.	5.
6.	6.
7.	7.
8.	8.
9.	9.
10.	10.

The things you like to do are easy for you and therein lies your talent. If you like to cook, you obviously have a talent for concocting good things to eat. If you like to dance, that rhythm you feel springs from your talent. If you like to do publicity for your club, you have a talent for writing and/or promotion.

Now look down the left-hand column. If you dislike driving a car, you have no feeling for machines. If you dislike babysitting, you do not relate well to small children and may even be afraid of the responsibility.

Respect your dislikes and likes, and you will begin to recognize your talent. Then you will be led into work that is stimulating in every way and completely right for you.

The difference between work and employment

"With your work," says John Ciardi, of *Saturday Review,* "the doing is itself the goal. Employment is undertaken for such reasons outside itself as pay, medical benefits, and whatever pensions may accrue."

At this stage, concentrate on what you like to do and forego whenever possible those chores that aren't related to this preference, which you can begin to think of now as your work. From now on, accept employment only if it gives you a chance to do this work. If you are lucky, this work of yours may bring in money, but don't start this time with money in mind. Consider only work you have a talent for. Everything else will come.

18

WORK AS A VOLUNTEER AND FEEL YOUR TALENT GROW

"Your enemy is apathy," warned Dorothy Flechtner, Director of Women's Activities in Public Affairs for the United States Chamber of Commerce, when she counted from a show of hands at a recent empty-nest symposium only 40 out of a group of 650 women who had ever worked actively for a political party. "Go to work for a cause you believe in," she urged, "and any talent you have will grow." This is a switch from the old "do good, and you will feel good" appeal to volunteers which many women no longer believe.

"The last time I answered a call for help," one frustrated woman told me, "I spent five days typing envelopes without ever being able to find out what was going into them or why. It was just so much hard work, and I didn't feel good about this at all."

Advice from a full-time volunteer

One of a vanishing breed, Mrs. Joseph Kirchheimer, a full-time volunteer in New York City and the only woman to receive a Certificate of Appreciation from the city's thirty-five-year-old Housing Authority, believes she knows why full-time volunteers are dying out.

"Today, empty nesters who can afford to work as full-time volunteers," she reasons, "believe that they can get more satisfaction from starting a business of their own or working for a paycheck and maybe doing a few hours of volunteering on the side." She regrets this and feels that women can get equal or more satisfaction from full-time volunteering, "if only they would take the time to find the kind of work that truly interests them."

Self-analysis is the key

"Not everyone likes the same kind of work," says Mrs. Kirchheimer. "The woman who feels threatened by close contact with ill health or a reminder of death will be upset if she is asked to work directly with hospital patients or the aged. But this does not automatically mean that she will work well with children. She may prefer the big picture—planning, coordinating, policy-making—rather than direct contact of any kind."

Before agreeing to do any volunteer work, Mrs. Kirchheimer, who is the initiator of Project Pilot, which provides help for aged individuals living alone on New York's West Side, recommends self-analysis. "Find a field that you are interested in, and you will be productive," she says. "Take an assignment that is wrong for you, and you will be upset or bored. Self-analysis is the key."

Exercise for your talent

If for nothing more than exercise for your talent, call your local Community Chest, Red Feather Referral Service, or your county's Volunteer Bureau and ask for a choice of jobs.* Or call the director of volunteers at your hospital.† She may give you a choice of working in the library, coffee shop, main office, or a nurse's station. Or maybe she will suggest that you serve as a receptionist, a patient escort, or a play therapist on the children's floor. If you want direct contact with patients, you will be given a short patient-care course to learn how to feed patients, make beds, give backrubs. Take to this and you will soon be happily at work in your cherry-red American Hospital Association pinafore, and your social life will have perked up, too, for in most hospitals you will be a member of the service and fund-raising auxiliary that sponsors the volunteer program.

Do not confuse volunteer hospital work with that of a nurse's aide, which is paid for in most hospitals at an hourly rate of about two dollars and takes longer preparation (usual training period, four to six weeks; pay during training, sixty-six dollars a week; education needed, high school).

Either your hospital or local Red Cross chapter will conduct the course you will take when you volunteer to work in a hospital. Call Red Cross direct, however, when

* In Arizona last winter, Maricopa County's Volunteer Bureau gave a friend of mine her choice of driving an emotionally disturbed child to a Child Guidance Center for treatment twice a week; serving as a teacher's aide in a Head Start agency (or lending a hand there with babies); typing envelopes for an unnamed agency; or collecting donated blankets and pans for recently discharged hospital patients who were setting up housekeeping. Her ambition is to write children's books, so she headed for Head Start.
† Not all hospital jobs call for direct contact with patients.

volunteering to work as a Gray Lady (either in a local or military hospital) or as a blood-donor aide, a much needed volunteer in most communities. Before being assigned to a bloodmobile, you will be trained with other volunteers in an all-day session. Once on the job, you will assist nurses, do clerical work, register donors and/or prepare food for the Red Cross canteen.

You may be urged to take pay

Understaffed schools welcome volunteers, but many urge women to accept the going rate of approximately $1.75 an hour as a teacher's aide rather than to work for free. (Lack of promptness and absenteeism make for crises in a tight school program, and educators say there is less of both when helpers take pay.) As a teacher's aide, you may be asked to work in the library, supervise study halls or the playground, help a teacher with paper work, stenciling, collecting money for lunches and programs, and/or shepherding small children in and out of coat rooms and the bus. In some schools, you will work on a one-to-one basis with students who are falling behind, but do not confuse this work with that of a substitute teacher, who must be a college graduate and in some states, a licensed teacher. (There are no educational or age specifications for teachers' aides.) For information about the particular needs of your school system, call the office of your superintendent of schools.

Ever wonder why a boy drops out of school? Talk to one. Offer on your own to be his tutor if he will give school one more try. If he's black and feels left out, get his white classmates to encourage him to stay. Or, if you are more emotionally in tune with small children, call your local Head Start office and offer to help disadvantaged white and black preschoolers catch up with the other kids before they hit first grade.

If you are over sixty, become a foster grandparent to a handicapped or disabled child in a local hospital or center either for pay or as a volunteer. Your assignment: to visit, read to, and love this child as you do your grandchildren. Your pay if your income is less than $1,500 a year: $1.60 an hour for twenty hours a week. If your income is higher than this (or your age is lower than sixty), you can work as a volunteer. For full information, call your Community Council, which encourages participation in this program in sixty-three American cities.

Do you like books?

Your public library probably has need for both professional and clerical workers. (The difference: professionals include director, heads of various departments, children's librarian, researchers. Clerks take care of book processing, book repairs, records, typing, filing, and the telephone.) If you have your college degree and want a top library job, get your master's degree now in library science. If you cannot qualify as a professional but like books and people who read, offer to do clerical work. (Going rate: $1.50 to $2.00 an hour.) Like schools, most libraries prefer to pay for help.

What about conservation?

You may not know what to do, but surely you are worried about the pollution of our rivers, streams and air, the dying out of specific species of birds and flowers, the disappearance of chestnut trees, the dying of our elms, and the lack of concern of developers for the beauty of this country.

Offer to help your local United States Soil and Conservation office or the state or county office with a worthwhile project. You may be asked to get a group of women together to tag all the different types of trees in your section of town, to catalogue spring wild flowers in a nearby woods, or to work with a group to clean up a trail. (One woman in Danbury, Connecticut, with the help of local Brownies, changed a town dumping place to a park.)

Get involved in town affairs

Take an active interest in town, state, and national politics. Join the League of Women Voters. *Get involved.* Study your local zoning laws. Do they need revising? Talk to your town leaders, your chamber of commerce, your friends. Work because you believe in something. Is an old landmark being torn down? Save it. Dig into its history, get all the facts to your newspaper, interest your local historical society. Is your crime rate going up? Do what deeply troubled women in the city of Indianapolis did, start an anticrime crusade!

Led by Mrs. Margaret Moore, a petite, gray-haired grandmother and one-time Mother of the Year, fifty thousand Indianapolis women, outraged by the murder of a ninety-year-old former teacher during a purse-snatch, made national headlines with their crusade. Dedicated women staged "knit-ins" to stop loitering in the parks and to bring better police protection, conducted classes for dropouts, and helped parolees reenter community life, As a result, Indiana's soaring crime rate slowed down and the Indianapolis movement has become a national one.

Growth comes when you get involved

Your talent expands when you use it, and growth comes when you become interested in something bigger than yourself. Look out instead of in and your whole personality changes. Your husband will be the first to see, and through exposure to your new interest, he, too, may become involved. As he approaches and crosses over to full-time retirement, this will be a delight to you and him, too.

A personal experience

Last year, Russ Butera, coordinator of community services of RESCUE* in Bridgewater, invited my husband and me to a noonday meeting of fifty Connecticut artists† and one hundred educators from eighteen nearby communities. At lunch, teachers and principals outlined specific educational and cultural needs of neighboring schools which they believed local artists could help to fill.

As a result, Cle and I conducted a course in "How to Write a Children's Book" for nine hundred 7th- and 8th-grade students at Danbury Junior High. In our five-session course,‡ we stressed one approach: Start with a basic idea and let your writing and art come from the core. Those with low grades as well as those with high grades responded with a creative output that amazed their teachers. Many who had done nothing before but "hack around" came up with illustrated stories good enough to publish.

Our pay of five hundred dollars for conducting the course

* Regional Educational Services Concept through United Effort.
† Artists, photographers, writers, cartoonists, puppeteers, film makers, musicians, etc.
‡ Six classes of 150 students in the auditorium per day for five sessions.

was small, but our delight in seeing our simple suggestions come back as stories we couldn't possibly have dreamed up made the whole experience worthwhile. When an opportunity comes to put our mutual abilities to work in another project we believe in, we will repeat.

See the world as volunteers

Should your husband become restless during a sabbatical or a long leave of absence or in retirement (before or after sixty-five), consider an away-from-home assignment for mature volunteers. In such projects, you usually are given travel expenses, food and housing, medical care, a small daily allowance and some banked pay, plus the chance to put your learned skills to work in a new part of the world. Here are some possibilities:

1. THE PEACE CORPS

No matter what your age, you can qualify if you are an American citizen, have a skill to offer, and can pass a simple physical examination. At the last count, 175 volunteers over fifty years of age—5 of them over seventy—were serving the Corps in Africa, Asia, and Latin America. Of this group, 69 were in the sixty-one to seventy age bracket; the oldest was an eighty-year-old nurse in Turkey.*

Needed skills range from teachers, engineers, doctors, and nurses to carpenters, farmers, fishermen, plumbers, and bulldozer operators. You don't have to be a college graduate or highly trained. A normal tour, including a ten- to twelve-week training course at an American college or university, lasts from twenty-four to twenty-seven months.

* A husband and wife will be assigned to the same project, and the Corps also needs single men and women. Physical standards are flexible.

For complete information, write to Peace Corps, Washington, D. C. 20526. Or ask at your post office for the name of the regional office nearest you and talk in person with a recruiter.

Financial thought for an over sixty-five couple living in their own home on Social Security: Rent your home furnished for your two-year stint. Bank the rent, which does not count as income against your Social Security allowance. Because your living will be paid for, you can bank your Social Security checks or take the money with you to buy foreign gifts for your family or to pay for extras you may want above your daily living allowance. Upon your return, you will receive $1,800 per person from the Peace Corp for two years' work. This $900 a year income is not enough to take anything away from your Social Security income,* so you will be able to put $3,600 in your joint bank account.

2. VISTA

Sometimes called the domestic Peace Corps, VISTA sends workers to economically depressed areas with the aim of helping impoverished Americans to help themselves. Volunteers teach adult education courses, develop community-action programs, register voters, and work as teacher assistants in preschool and day-care centers. They work on Indian reservations, in urban ghettos, in mental health institutions, in isolated rural areas in the South, and in Alaskan fishing villages.

There is a special need for volunteers with specific skills —lawyers, planners, architects, medical personnel, business consultants—who are given six weeks of training where they work in conditions similar to those they will find on

---

* You can earn $1,680 per year and still receive maximum Social Security benefits.

the job in a poor community. Volunteers receive medical and personal expenses and a meager daily living allowance, plus fifty dollars a month (which is paid in a lump sum at the end of service, usually a one-year term). Today, one out of five VISTA volunteers is retired, and some workers are in their eighties. For specific information, write to VISTA, Office of Economic Opportunity, Washington, D.C. 20506.

3. INTERNATIONAL EXECUTIVE SERVICE CORPS

As a former high-level business executive, your husband or you may be eligible to serve through the above organization as an unsalaried advisor on a short-term basis to a private company in an underdeveloped country. The foreign client pays travel expenses and on-the-job living expenses for two, amounting to one thousand dollars a month or better, for which the volunteer does not pay taxes. The assignment: to provide hard-nosed managerial counsel to a foreign business. The names of several thousand would-be volunteers are now on file, and matching a volunteer with a specific job is a highly selective process, so your chance of being tapped for a job is not as probable as with the Peace Corps. But if you are called, the rewards are great. For an application blank, write to I.E.S.C., 545 Madison Avenue, New York, New York 10020.

ALTERNATE SUGGESTION: VITA

VITA, the Volunteers for Technical Assistance, Inc., headquartered in Schenectady, New York, uses American professionals to provide solutions to technological problems in underdeveloped nations. Advice in this case goes by mail.

Look back at your list on page 122

You have now read many suggestions for serving at home and elsewhere as a volunteer. If one avenue interests you, go back to page 122 and check this interest against what you like to do in everyday life. Will this new work bring into play at least five of the everyday activities you enjoy? If so, volunteer now. You will do well.

If your husband is still working full time, he can't get away for a long-time volunteer project and may have no time to work with you on a joint project in your community. Should you be tempted but timid about taking your first step as a volunteer alone, join a women's service organization and serve as a member of a group.

Your choice of seventeen service groups

The national organizations listed below are dedicated to arousing citizen interest in public affairs, providing community service, and in pioneering new fields of adult education. All have state-wide representation. Read down the list for one in which you will find a built-in compatibility with other members.

1. American Association of University Women
2. American Farm Bureau Federation Women's Committee
3. American Legion Auxiliary
4. Association of Junior Leagues of America, Inc.
5. B'nai B'rith Women
6. Business and Professional Women's Club
7. Church Women United
8. General Federation of Women's Clubs

9. Girl Scouts of the U.S.A.
10. League of Women Voters of the United States
11. National Association of Colored Women's Clubs
12. National Congress of Parents and Teachers
13. National Council of Catholic Women
14. National Council of Jewish Women
15. Soroptimist Federation of the Americas, Inc.
16. Young Women's Christian Association of the U.S.A.
17. Zonta International

In addition to these groups, your church guild, thrift shop, community center, and a dozen other organizations need any help you can give.

Unique service bureau

So far as I know, the Service Bureau for Women's Organizations, with offices at G. Fox and Company Building in Hartford, Connecticut, and supported by the Beatrice Fox Auerbach Foundation, is unique. Its purpose: to assist women's organizations functioning in Connecticut to be more effective in communities in the state where their particular service projects are needed. Members of its cooperating committee are appointed by the Connecticut branch of the national organizations listed above. The Service Bureau was established to encourage citizen participation in public affairs and to pioneer in techniques of adult education. The Service Bureau, directed by Mrs. Chase Going Woodhouse, never competes; rather, it implements, coordinates, and expedites work being done by member organizations in developing leadership among their members and in implementing their programs for community improvement.

The story of FISH

Volunteers for FISH* work on a person-to-person basis as needed to transport patients to clinics and hospitals, provide emergency babysitting service, visit shut-ins, read to older people, etc. Begun in England, the idea for a FISH group was brought to Massachusetts, then caught on in town after town along the east coast. To begin, list an answering service where those who need help can call and those with time to volunteer can respond. For complete information, write to: Mrs. Sylvester Craig, Box 381, New Milford, Connecticut.

Need for seasoned understanding

Many problems connected with child-care and old-age assistance have an emotional basis, so any solution has to be thought out with patience and wisdom. This is where your seasoned understanding, harnessed to your talent, can have far-reaching influence for others and for you.

---

* According to FISH volunteers, early Christians put the sign of the fish on their homes to signify that they were believers; this group simply adopted the symbol.

19

NOW IS THE TIME
TO GO BACK TO SCHOOL

Mothers of grown children go back to school for one of three reasons: (1) to finish an interrupted high school or college course; (2) to take a short-term life-enriching class in art or music appreciation, history or literature; (3) to prepare for special volunteer or commercial work. By far the greatest number go for reason number three, either to qualify for a program like Peace Corps, a specific city's School Volunteer Program,* or for part-time office work.

Fill out an application to work for the Red Cross, your local hospital, or a temporary employment service, and you will be told what training or brush-up course is required. Head for a career on your own and you will have to seek out courses that are right for you. Never fear that they

---

* New York City's Board of Education conducts a series of five training sessions per month during the school year for volunteers who will be working as reading helpers, teachers of conversational English, classroom assistants, conductors of roving "Museums on Wheels," and traveling libraries. Information available from: School Volunteer Program, 20 W. 40th Street, New York, N. Y. 10018.

won't be available. There is no career for which you can't find training, if you are really serious.

All kinds of schools

Look under "Schools" in the classified section of your telephone directory, and you will be amazed at the number of places that give lessons in dancing, drama, dressmaking, dog training, driving, elocution, flying, golf, horseback riding, knitting, modeling, music, sewing, speech correction, swimming, or special tutoring. There are few subjects that you may be interested in for which you cannot find instruction close at home.

Naturally, you aren't going to say, "Now I'm going back to school," and go eenie-meenie down the yellow page to make your selection. The way the list is expanding you can end up in anything from baton twirling to hypnosis, either of which might be fun, but only if it ties in with what you want to do next. First step is your goal; then comes the school.

Special training for a special goal

Are you a good photographer who would like to become professional? Take a home study course from the Famous Photographers School in Westport, Connecticut, or some similar organization. You can take three years to complete assignments with the help of a personal counselor and clear do-it-yourself materials prepared with the help of ten top professionals.* The cost of the course runs about twenty-

* Richard Avedon, Richard Beattie, Joseph Costa, Arthur d'Arazien, Alfred Eisenstaedt, Harry Garfield, Philippe Halsman, Irving Penn, Bert Stern, Ezra Stoller.

two dollars a month for a full-term home-instruction plan.

Want to learn typing and shorthand so that you can help your husband with a book he is writing or in a new business he is considering? Call your local superintendent of schools or recreation centers and ask where to sign up for instruction through your town's adult education program. Most communities have two or three ten-to-twelve session programs a year; cost for a course runs about one dollar per session or less. Programs in most communities offer everything from lessons in Spanish (which you may be interested in if your husband has an assignment a year from now in Madrid) to food management (a good first step if you are thinking of buying an inn). Courses in most cases do not count as credits in a college program; they do provide an excellent self-enrichment opportunity in exchange for a minimum of time and money.

More courses than you know

Would you like to match people with houses? Your eventual field may be real estate. To qualify for a license to be a saleswoman or broker, you will have to pass a state exam. Write to your state Real Estate Board in your capital city for your state's study, training, and apprenticeship requirements; get the book recommended as background for your state exam, and read, read, read.* Ask your state board where special courses are available near you. Some real estate associations sponsor courses for newcomers.

Are you a one-time biology major who would like to get into research? Go to graduate school at a nearby college. Want to be a stockbroker? Take an adult education course

* Connecticut Board's recommendation: Robert Semenow's *Questions and Answers on Real Estate,* Englewood Cliffs, Prentice-Hall, 1966.

in investments; later, become a trainee in a brokerage house, taking a correspondence course from the New York Stock Exchange as you work. Want to write for magazines at home? Take a night course in creative writing or a correspondence course through Famous Schools or the Palmer Writers School in Minneapolis. Want to speak French? Call Berlitz.*

Do you have a feeling for color, a flair for fashion, a delight in home decoration? Call your local Fashion Group (the dress buyer for that elegant local store of yours is a member) and ask if experts will be giving a fashion career course near you.

As a member of The Fashion Group in New York, I received a reminder today that our thirty-second annual career course for newcomers and mature executives in the fashion industry will soon begin. Cost of the course is twenty dollars, which pays for two-hour evening lectures by dedicated speakers on ten consecutive Tuesdays, featuring such experts as Adele Simpson (designing and manufacturing); Coulette Touhey, from Bergdorf Goodman (merchandising); Kathryne Hays, from *Vogue* (accessories); Letitia Baldrige (public relations). The Fashion Group has affiliated groups in cities like Minneapolis, San Francisco, and Kansas City. Check to see if the group near you is sponsoring a career course. If not, get a job, any kind of a job, working close to one of your town's top fashion women and learn the business that way. And, by all means, if you happen to be spending a couple of fall months in New York in any year, sign up for the career course through The Fashion Group, Inc., 6 Rockefeller Plaza, New York, New York 10020.

An advertising communications course somewhat similar in format to The Fashion Group career course has recently

---

* Cost for two-month course for one in a group of ten, $140.

been announced by Advertising Women of New York. If you are a writer who wants to do copy writing for an agency, radio station, department store, or newspaper in your town, check with a member of your local Ad Club to see if such a course is offered near you. Far more opportunities of this nature are available than most women know.

Self-improvement classes

If your life has been tied up with the children for many years, you probably lack the self-confidence to move out now to new pursuits, no matter how stimulating.

Unqualified recommendation: a Dale Carnegie or Dorothy Carnegie course. Cost is in the neighborhood of two hundred dollars for a twelve-session series of four-hour classes. Results are amazing. Timid, white-faced people who cannot address the group without clutching a table and being flanked by students and others at the first session emerge at the end of the course as smiling speakers who can talk easily about anything on or off stage. Dale Carnegie night courses are for men and women; Dorothy Carnegie courses, which may take place in afternoons, are for women only. Either is worthwhile.

Other confidence-builders: course at a John Roberts Powers or other charm school; makeup instruction and a complete do at an Elizabeth Arden, Helena Rubenstein, or Revlon salon or from an Avon representative; dancing lessons at Arthur Murray or Fred Astaire studios; grooming classes in a prejob training course often given by a temporary employment service; studio voice lessons; modeling class for possible television career.*

Also extremely helpful: bridge classes, yoga sessions,

---

* Don't laugh, even if you're over seventy. Little old ladies are the darlings of copywriters today—command big fees.

golf and tennis instruction, and/or drama classes that bring you into contact with others as you learn.

Preparation helps for a business of your own

Want to own your own beauty shop? First step: take a course in beauty culture at a licensed school. Before signing up, check state requirements to work for another and for yourself.

Thinking of buying a flower shop or running your own nursery? Talk to conservationists about local soil conditions, take an adult education or special college course in horticulture, learn garden planning and flower arranging at your local craft center or through your garden club.

Want to have a cooking school some day? Sign up for a gourmet cooking class. Thinking of buying a motel or resort hotel? Write to International Training Systems, Inc., 1457 Broadway, New York, New York, and ask for full information about home study course for hotel managers. Study as you search.

Can you earn money as a dressmaker or designer? Begin with a good basic sewing course offered by a local vocational school or the Singer Sewing Machine Company. Then, go on to a nearby school of design or your local fashion academy. Or get a job with the best women's tailor or milliner or designer in your town and learn on the job.

You have plenty of time to do just about anything you want to do, so don't hold back because of your age, but do take advantage of all the training opportunities you can manage. You may rise to the top even if you were a sixth-grade dropout; but get more schooling. In most cases, the more training you have the higher your income will be.

No high-school diploma?

If you didn't finish high school, get an equivalency diploma through your state's GEDT* program. No special instruction needed if you can pass basic multiple-choice tests in five high-school subjects (English, Literature, Social Studies, Science, and Math). Exams take ten hours, are given in two five-hour Saturday sessions. Apply at your local high school; total cost: three dollars. Should you get a below-passing grade in any subject, sign up for special evening instruction through your local Board of Education's adult education program. Retake your GEDT exam when ready. Most jobs of any stature require a high-school diploma, and college is impossible without one, so get yours now this streamlined way.

College interrupted?

If you left college before getting your degree, you can finish now, but you may have some unforeseen hurdles to get over, even to get in. Some colleges and universities allow no credits for correspondence courses or courses taken more than seven years ago, and few give credit for work graded below C. Biggest problem: Most colleges require the final thirty hours of credit to be earned on campus.† Before making any decision to go or not to go back, write to your former college for credits and grades and take this

* General Education Development and Training program.
† This means that if you live far from where you went to college and have only seventeen hours to go, you have to repeat thirteen hours as well as take seventeen new hours from a new school to graduate. Many modern educators object, saying that in today's fluid world married women can't bank on spending thirty hours on one campus. Thus there is hope that the rule will be changed.

record to the admissions office of your nearest college or university. If you learn that a year of hard work will get you a degree, enroll. Attend classes for a year, and you will find out what you are truly interested in. Later, with your B.A. behind you, you can go on for graduate work, if you wish.

Off-campus study possibilities

Several years ago, Goddard College at Plainfield, Vermont, pioneered an off-campus adult degree program that has served as a pattern for similar programs now offered by five or six other colleges and universities.

In the Goddard Adult Degree Program, you spend only two weeks out of every six months on campus and do the rest of your work at home under the careful guidance of an on-campus advisor. When you complete the required work, you are granted a B.A. degree that is identical to the Bachelor of Arts degree earned by Goddard students completing undergraduate work on campus. The work during any six months' period, however, is quite different from that done for regular college courses.

In your first two weeks on campus, you will build with the help of the faculty a six months' work project around a subject which deeply interests you and which will demand enough independent study to count for a semester's credit toward your degree. When you complete a semester's project to your satisfaction and that of your advisor, you will return to Goddard to do advance planning for your next semester.

As a rule, at Goddard you are given credit for courses taken in the past in any recognized liberal arts college or university in which you earned C or above.* However, when

* Occasionally, someone with no credits for college work is given credit for a year of advance standing in the Goddard program if he

you enroll, you must plan to spend a minimum of three se-
mesters in the Goddard program. Although present costs may
eventually go up, today's tuition for a six-month semester at
Goddard is only $650, and the cost of room and board
for each two week's session on campus is only $150. This
program is certainly worth looking into if you can't get the
credits you need for your degree nearby or live far from a
college or university. For complete details, write to the
Adult Degree Program Office, Goddard College, Plainfield,
Vermont 05667.

Start from scratch in Oklahoma program

If you have a high school diploma (or equivalency certificate) you can take as long as you want to complete college
courses off-campus for B.L.S. degree* from the University of
Oklahoma. Many women complete their guided study projects under this plan as they work in their home towns as
volunteers or in part-time or full-time jobs. Oklahoma's program concentrates on three areas: humanities, social sciences, and like the Goddard plan, it calls for some on-campus
work (four on-campus seminars in all). Because of its unusual flexibility, the overall cost for several years of schooling at Oklahoma is low. Count on total fees of approximately
$2,150 (plus living expenses during seminars) for however
long it takes you to earn your degree. For full details write
to the College of Continuing Education, University of
Oklahoma, Norman, Oklahoma 73069.†

---

or she has an outstanding record in terms of self-education and/or
professional success and scores well in College Level Examination
tests.

* Bachelor of Liberal Studies

† A few adults with unusually rich experience and prior learning may
complete this course in two years or less; the average adult with the
educational equivalent of a high school graduation should figure on

Figure travel costs as you plan

As you add up the expenses involved in any self-study plan that calls for on-campus sessions, you naturally will have to figure in travel costs. Because two cross-country trips a year can run high, you will be wise to enroll at a school within driving or easy plane or train commuting distance. Excellent programs, for instance, are offered by both the University of South Florida and by Syracuse University. If you live near Tampa, you will naturally go there rather than north; if you live in New York State, you will be wise to enroll at Syracuse.

South Florida's program is much like Oklahoma's B.L.S. program; in fact, the curriculum and approach are similar enough to warrant transfer of work done from one to the other on a reciprocal basis. So if you like the description of the Oklahoma program but live closer to Tampa (or can dovetail an occasional trip to the campus with a planned business or vacation trip to Florida with your husband), write for details to Kevin E. Kearney, Ph.D., Director, Adult Degree Program, University of South Florida, Tampa, Florida 33620. The overall cost will run about the same as at Oklahoma.

The nonresidential bachelor's degree program offered by Syracuse is available to anyone of any age with a high school diploma or its equivalent who can pass the required entrance tests. A Bachelor of Arts Degree in Liberal Studies is conferred when you complete work on four levels (or have been given credit courses taken previously) in these four areas: humanities, science, social science, mathematics.

Overall costs ($1,300 tuition for each level plus books and food and lodging while attending campus seminars) are

---

four years. Once you get your bachelor's degree through this program or another, you are eligible for a similar off-campus degree program in the graduate college at Oklahoma.

higher than at Goddard, Oklahoma, or South Florida, but financial aid through the National Defense Education Act may be available. Under this Act, a student can borrow up to one thousand dollars a year for five years with no interest charge until after graduation, when 3 percent interest is charged as repayment is made in ten annual installments. For full details about the Syracuse program, write to Thomas Benzel, Director, Program for Liberal Studies, University of Syracuse, Syracuse, New York 13202.

Opportunities for home economists

Last year, empty nesters back for a second go at school at Purdue University in West Lafayette, Indiana, visited me by telephone*—their field: home economics, their questions: What opportunities are available to home economists wherever they live? What area of study do you recommend as a partner to home economics? Is the pay good? My answers:

1. Testing recipes for food companies, writing food ads, planning food photography, teaching home economics, planning menus for schools and hospitals, catering, helping individuals with home management, helping retailers in the fields of fashion and foods.

2. Combine home economics courses in this school with: economics, journalism, education, social welfare.

3. Pay is excellent, with more jobs available than trained women can fill.

---

* Women in adult education courses in home economics watched in the university's Memorial Union as slides of me and my home were flashed on screen. By long-distance telephone, they asked and I answered questions about opportunities in their field. My voice was amplified so all could hear.

Select the field of home economics as a profession, and all your instincts and experience as a woman will come into play.

Continuum Center in Michigan

With the help of a grant from the Kellogg Foundation, Oakland University in Rochester, Michigan, has developed a novel Continuum Center for women. In three years, more than fourteen hundred women have paid a fee of eighty-five dollars (only half of the cost of the services provided) for an individual assessment program which includes psychological and career preference testing and advice from a professional on future plans for education, volunteer service, and/or employment. One major aim: to help women work toward a constructive future when the mothering years end.

Only a few examples

Examples in this chapter of opportunities available to mature women just scratch the surface. Investigate your local adult education courses and you will find a wide range of study possibilities. Visit three or four schools and colleges in your state, and you will be flabbergasted at each one's interest in continuing education for adults and the cooperation you receive. Chances are you will be able to find a continuing project that you can pursue without leaving home. Investigate and decide which approach is right for you. And be glad you live today, when going back to school at any age is getting easier all the time.

20

GETTING PAID FOR WHAT
YOU LIKE TO DO

When you were growing up, the average employed woman was single and twenty-eight years or younger; today, she is married and forty-one years or older. Soon, if you don't earn money for something you produce, you will be the exception. Already, in this country, 50 percent of all women aged forty-five to fifty-four are in the labor force, the highest percentage of any age group; and four out of ten women over fifty-five are money earners. Goodbye to the babushka-type grandma. In this country, more than a million part-time workers now earn close to a billion dollars a year; and among them there are more working grandmothers than just plain working mothers!

When John J. Husic, who has encouraged this trend, was president of the Institute of Temporary Services, he told me there was a logical two-way reason for the mature woman's going to work. "Alone now, she appreciates the opportunity to get out of the house, mix with people, be productive, and earn money. And the harried executive appreciates her dedication to what he has to get done and her steadiness. Over the years, her day-by-day experience in running a home has left her with a built-in ability to cope with on-the-job physical and emotional stress."

Today's employers, John Husic believes, far prefer the older woman with common sense to her mini-skirted daughter with marriage, pregnancy, and/or unreliable baby-sitters on her mind. Certainly if you want to work for pay, neither your age nor your sex will be a handicap. All you have to do is decide what you want to do and do it.

Business wants you

If you want work immediately, look in the yellow pages of your telephone book under "Employment Contractors —Temporary" and call Employers Overload, Kelly Girl, Manpower, Western Girl, or a similar service.* Within days, you can go out on your first job, with or without a brush-up course, depending on your former experience and the kind of job you want. Here are fields open to women where the demand for both permanent or temporary employees always exceeds the supply.

    Clerical work: Stenographers, typists, secretaries, cashiers, grocery checkers, telephone operators, bookkeepers, receptionists, file clerks, library assistants, telephone ad takers, survey enumerators, office machine operators, proofing machine operators.

    Saleswork: Increasing need for retail sales people in suburban stores provides a new employment opportunity near home for the woman who likes to sell.

    Service work: Waitresses, hostesses, beauty operators, practical nurses, elevator operators, cleaning

---

* Two myths keep some women from doing this: (1) A temporary services agency takes a third of your pay in commission. (False. The employer pays the agency on top of what the agency pays you. You get full pay.) (2) The world wants youth. (False. Business wants you.)

women, ushers, school-crossing patrolers, and meter maids.

Operatives: Usually, in manufacturing and processing plants—which doesn't mean a "Rosie, the Riveter" job—the need is for package fillers, machine supervisors, etc.; the category also includes dressmakers and seamstresses, bus and taxi drivers, streetcar conductors, and laundry and dry-cleaning operators.

Private household workers: Some women prefer to work for others rather than at home.

Professional, technical and kindred occupations: teachers, librarians, nurses, dietitians, dental hygienists, medical technologists, medical X-ray technicians, social workers.

If money is what you want

The more schooling you have, the more you will be inclined to work outside of your home; and the more training you have, the more money you will earn. According to the United States Department of Labor, 80 percent of all women aged thirty-five to fifty-four with a college background are now in the labor force, and their per capita earnings far outdistance that of women with a high-school diploma only. So if money is what you want, go on with your education even as you work.

Enlarging your life

"Education," says social psychologist Kurt Lewin, "enlarges the life space." Reach for a better job through special on-the-job training or through adult education or in a college program, and you will be doing far more than going to a few classes or acquiring more credits toward a degree. You will be changing your perspective, whetting your curiosity for more learning, enlarging your life space. Whatever job you start out with will soon be outgrown; you will automatically move up.

Write your own ticket

If what you want now is to work a week or two every month, saving time out for long summer and winter vacations, you can pretty much write your own ticket about where and when you work (with no penalty for stay-out time) if you begin work through one of the temporary-help services. Later, when you find yourself becoming interested in a particular type of work, you may want to work full time.

Talk about what you want to do

You may know exactly what you want to do but may feel a little timid when it comes to talking about it. Suppose, for instance, a friend of yours has recently opened a contemporary gift shop a few miles from your home. You are a potter or work in stitchery or are experimenting with a new fabric-designing process, and you want to talk to your friend about selling your work, but you hesitate for fear she will think you expect a favor.

Go ahead. You aren't in grade school anymore, or at a tea, either. Call your friend tomorrow, but be businesslike. Ask her if you can bring samples of your work to the shop so she can see what you are doing. Or suggest that she stop by your home where she can see your work in quantity.

Ask her, and expect to hear, whether she thinks your

work will sell, how much she can afford to pay you per item so that she can make the profit she wants, whether she will let you put your work in her shop on consignment. Listen carefully for any suggestions she has about revising your work so it will go. You may decide the deal she offers isn't for you; she may decide your work isn't anything she can sell. But talking will help you in many ways.

Whenever you decide what you want to do, make it a rule to talk about it, not at dinner parties or by buttonholing your friends in corners, but in a straightforward businesslike way by appointment, or when a specific opportunity you have been waiting for presents itself.

Go to an expert

Don't go to your sister who lives on a farm to talk about what to do to get a job in an exclusive dress shop in your state capital. Save your energy, because she can't help. Go to her to find out the cost of land in her county; but as a forerunner to applying at the dress shop, talk to a friend of your husband's who sells to the woman you want to work for, or to someone who buys from her, or to a newspaper reporter in her town.

Don't ask Betty Crocker what stock to buy; ask a Wall Street man. Ask Betty Crocker how to bake a cake.

Make this a rule and you won't dissipate your energy talking to the wrong person. You will, however, talk to the right person whenever you are considering a course of action.

Suppose you want a full-time job tomorrow

The reason for the popularity of part-time work with empty nesters is that they do not have to commit themselves to a job before they know that it is what they want.

And employers like the arrangement, too. They do not have to break in new employees, handle application forms and paper work, fire an employee direct if she doesn't work out. Working through an agency often makes a lot of sense for both the employer and the employee.

There will be times, however, when an employer needs a full-time staff employee right away, and you want the job. Maybe you were a reporter on a good-sized newspaper in the early days of your marriage, but you haven't worked for years. Now you want to go back to work, and you know your local newspaper needs a society editor. In a case like this there is no point in going to anyone but the person who is doing the hiring. And if you know the editor or the publisher of the paper, and he knows you, so much the better. Go to him, but once again, do be businesslike.

The best course is to write a short letter saying that you know about the job, want it, and that you have had five, six, or ten years' experience on a newspaper. Tell him that you are well acquainted with the social activities in your city, which he probably knows. End by saying that you will call for an appointment in two days. Then, do it.

Follow this same procedure whenever you know you are qualified and a job is available. When you are answering an ad in the paper, make these three points: (1) you want the job; (2) there are good reasons why you should have it; (3) you will call for an appointment. Be brief, be direct, be there.

How to hide your age when applying

"Don't try," say employment counselors. "An old wedding date or graduation year is bound to trip you up." Their suggestion: "Be the most attractive and competent-looking woman you can be; no one after your first interview will ask your age or think about it." And fashion experts say:

Shorten your hair, slim down, dress simply, and go easy on your makeup. "You are going to work, not a party." Keep your hat and your lips turned up, be perfectly groomed always, and wear pink a lot. "Let the young girls be sexy; you be elegant."

Wanted: a business of your own

While working for others, you may decide that what you want is a business of your own. But you don't know whether you will do better with a nursery school or a dog kennel, an antique store or an auction barn, a dress shop or a flower market.* Talk to your Chamber of Commerce about local competition in the field you are considering, rents, possible locations, zoning restrictions. Then, as your goal becomes specific, call the Small Business Administration office nearest you, listed under United States Government, and ask for free counseling from a nearby member of SCORE (Service Corps of Retired Executives). If advised to go ahead, talk to SBA again about a possible loan. Assuming the business you are contemplating is not speculative (e.g., buying land for one price and selling at another) and you can't get all your capital from a bank, you can borrow up to 75 percent of what you need at 5.5 percent interest through a bank with SBA backing. See how a dream becomes a plan.

College-trained and not working?
Don't waste your talent

Knowing that America has two and a half million college-educated women who are not interested in a conventional job but whose talents are now underused, a nonprofit organization has come up with a novel plan. Called Cata-

* Or any of a dozen other businesses.

lyst (6 East 82nd Street, New York, New York 10028), its purpose is to place women in part-time positions in education, science, industry, and social work. Contacted recently by the Massachusetts Department of Welfare, it recruited, trained, and supervised fifty women to fill twenty-five full-time caseworker jobs. It also cooperates with colleges in experimental campus-linked home study and part-time teaching programs which lead to teacher certification. Two booklets for would-be part-time teachers are available on request.

If you are trained in any line, *do something*. Work, like education, will enlarge your frame of reference, so don't waste your talent. There's a big world waiting out there for the competent woman who has the time and the desire to contribute.

21

TWELVE WAYS TO EARN MONEY WITH THE TALENT THAT'S ALWAYS BEEN YOURS

I have earned money as a writer in at least twelve different fields. I have written books, ghosted books, had my own publicity agency, and written for another publicity agency. I have taught journalism in a university, worked out a how-to-write program for grade schools, and written articles for magazines for writers. I have promoted dozens of products and ideas, have supervised advertising for international clients, in both New York and Paris, and have produced new product ideas for research projects on both continents. And I have put my writing to work in seemingly unrelated fields like real estate. What I have done, you can do, whatever your work may be.

Five years ago, a friend of ours was talked into a state cooking contest, sponsored by a dairy association. Much to her surprise, she won the top cash prize for creating and baking a bacon and egg pie. Since then, she has sold her pies for private parties, made them for a delicatessen, taught others how to cook in a dairy-sponsored cooking school, demonstrated on stage how to make a flaky pie crust, worked out a how-to story for a newspaper, sold her Americanized recipe for *quiche Lorraine* for a cottage cheese promotion, appeared in a commercial as an expert cook, taken part in a research project for a giant food company, and baked her pie for noonday customers in her daughter's beauty shop.

Five years ago, our friend knew that she liked to cook, but she honestly didn't know that her creative ability in the kitchen was truly unusual. Today she knows what she can do, and her talent is going out in all directions. You can do the same with yours.

If you want to get a clearer idea of where your talent lies, read down the list "Money-making Avenues" on page 160 and consider all the possibilities for using your special aptitude in business. To get you started, see what others do.

Read how a typist, receptionist, and teacher can put their special skills to work in many fields. Never mind if your skill is not yet fully developed. See what you can do eventually when your talent is honed to a fare-thee-well.

And your well will never run dry

An ironing woman in our town talks about her work as her profession. She has a long waiting list of people who want her services, and she is in demand in our county when a wedding dress arrives late from New York, when linen napkins have to be done just so for a big dinner, when a local laundry gets a special job that calls for the very best. In a day of sloppy workmanship, her pride is good to see, and it pays off in money, constant involvement in community affairs, and a lack of boredom.

Your profession need not be what others call glamorous, but you must perform *well*. Then you will be happy in your work, and your well will never run dry.

Work and stay young

More than fifteen million women over forty-five, most of them married, are employed full time and are bringing home a giant share of the ninety billion dollars (hardly pin money) that women now earn annually. Due to new vocational and educational opportunities, women are starting important careers in their midforties and fifties and their inclination to do so is a significant reflection of their being "with it" in today's ageless society.

"Far from thinking that a woman's place is in the home, as her mother believed," says Dr. Jesse Barnard, sociologist, "today's woman under sixty welcomes the chance to realize an ambition she may have been stifling for years. The woman over sixty, however, may still consider such an ambition questionable."

Obviously, then, the way you feel about a woman's working reveals your years more than any other attitude you may express. No matter what your age, doing good work in a job you like is a far better way to keep young than to have a face-lift. And if this work of yours brings in more money than you ever believed possible, so much the better. Your career is an expression of youth.

Money-making Avenues	*Opportunities for a Typist*
1. Sell it "as is."	1. Type manuscripts at home for a price.
2. Stand in for another.	2. Fill in for another typist who is doing this same kind of work.
3. In a business you run.	3. Become the owner of a part-time employment service which types and supplies typists for businesses.
4. In a business run by another.	4. Work as a typist for a part-time employment service.
5. Teach it.	5. Teach typing in a business college.
6. Demonstrate how to do what you do.	6. Demonstrate advance-model typewriters for a manufacturer.
7. Write about it for pay.	7. Write a short-cut course for typists in the form of a teach-yourself manual.
8. Use it in promotion.	8. Demonstrate on TV and talk on radio and to newspaper reporters about a new typewriter in a manufacturer's promotion effort.
9. Use it in advertising.	9. Write advertising for a local business supply company or a national manufacturer.
10. Use it in research.	10. Help a research company find out what typists want in a typewriter.
11. Use it on the platform.	11. Talk to students taking secretarial courses about where this course can lead them. (Billy Rose became Bernard Baruch's secretary as a result of winning a typing contest, and went on from there as a promoter to become a millionaire.)
12. Use it as an asset in an unrelated business.	12. Type as part of your work in a newspaper or any other enterprise.

Opportunities for a Receptionist

1. Work as a part-time receptionist assigned by an agency.
2. Fill in for a friend on vacation who is a full-time receptionist.
3. Act as hostess in your husband's restaurant or in some other business.
4. Become the receptionist in a business office, real estate firm, or dental office.
5. Advise women going out on their first part-time jobs how and what to do.
6. Make up a set of rules to be used by part-time employment firms sending out receptionists.
7. Write a humorous article about your first day as a receptionist.
8. Show model homes to visitors in real estate development where you live.
9. Model as a receptionist in brochures or commercials or in newspaper ads which are selling the homes you are showing.
10. While acting as receptionist in your husband's restaurant, interview customers about preferences in food for a research project.
11. Take a public-speaking course and talk to women's clubs and other groups about your adventures as a receptionist.
12. Open a gift shop, antique shop, or other business where your background as a receptionist can come into play.

Opportunities for a Teacher

1. Teach in a public school.
2. Work as a substitute teacher.
3. Start a private nursery school or a day-care center.
4. Work as a teacher-editor in a correspondence school for writers, photographers, cooks, etc.
5. Teach in a teachers' college.
6. Start a how-to magazine for teachers in computer programming or some other new field.
7. Write for a teacher's magazine.
8. Give cooking classes for a food manufacturer.
9. Serve as advertising consultant for an agency trying to reach instructors. (Example: how to get teachers of cooking classes to use a given product.)
10. Conduct research in your private school or for a manufacturer of play equipment.
11. Explain new teaching methods to equipment manufacturers and book publishers.
12. Use teaching methods to break in salesman for your husband's real estate business or demonstrators for your own cosmetics firm.

22

WHAT FIRST?

As we know, when a woman enrolls in the College of Continuing Education at the University of Oklahoma, she studies in three broad areas, one after the other (Humanities, including fine arts, history, literature, philosophy, and religion; Social Sciences, including anthropology, psychology, sociology, economics, political science, history, and human geography; and Natural Science, including biological sciences, earth sciences, and physical sciences). Eventually, she completes work in all three areas, but she does her first project in the area where she has the greatest interest, which in her case is revealed in her placement tests.

You can follow the same procedure in deciding whether your first major outside effort as an empty nester should be made as a volunteer, a student, or a money earner. Begin in the area where you have your highest level of interest. This simple questionnaire will help you decide.

To find which one,
answer these nine questions—yes or no

A. 1. Have you served as a volunteer for anything in the last year in which you are tremendously interested?

2. As a rule, do you like women who do volunteer work better than women who play in bridge tournaments?

3. Can you name three conditions in your community that you feel should be changed? (Zoning, conservation neglect, dishonest town officials, segregation?)

B. 1. Did you love school as a child and are you good at "little tests?"

2. Is there some particular field that you would like to know a lot more about?

3. Are you a voluminous reader on any or every subject?

C. 1. Would you like to invest money in the stock market on your own without your husband's help?

2. Do you like to know in the morning what you will be doing six hours of the day?

3. Do you have a good job or know where you would like to have one?

Give yourself an A if you have three yes answers in the A section; B, if you have three yes answers in the B section; C, if you have three yes answers in the C section. Read advice below.

A—Start today as a volunteer. You have much to contribute on full- or part-time projects.

B—A born student, you should work for a degree (or advanced degree) in field that interests you. Teach later, perhaps.

C—You are a career woman and like money making as a game. Take courses related to work advancement.

AB—Combine volunteer work with study. Your thinking goes deeper than most, can lead to writing or government projects.

BC—You should have your own business, should be studying and working now to push up income.

AC—Start as money earner but volunteer for an after-hours project you believe in. You are efficient and can do both without neglecting your husband.

ABC—You do everything well, so it really doesn't matter where you begin. Best course, maybe: school with job in mind. Volunteer as you study; later volunteer as you work.

No letters (less than three yes answers in every section) —You like your home, will have to push to do much outside. Do take at least one course (if only flower arranging) that you really care about. Later, do occasional volunteering.

You eventually will do something in each area. But in the beginning, work in the one or two areas where your level of interest is high.

23

THE "BE" PRINCIPLE

"Every wish," wrote Elizabeth Barrett Browning, "is like a prayer." Now that you have begun to analyze what you do easily, you are becoming aware of your particular talent, and you only wish that you had begun long ago to do what you know you could have done. This kind of thinking will get you nowhere, but there's one kind of wishing (or praying) that will.

Decide right now that by six months from today you will be doing something new that puts your talent to work as never before. This can be something productive that you will do for money, as a volunteer, in a club, with a new group of friends, in your home, as you travel, anything. But the decision must be to do something *new* that springs from your talent, and this new effort must reflect your personal growth.

Be ready and be there

Let's say that you are working in your first temporary job as a typist in a pool in a large office. You have had a brush-up course through the agency that placed you, and, now as

165

you type, you find that you are far faster and more efficient than others in the pool. "If I were just younger," you say to yourself, "I could go far in business."

You are right. As a born manager, you should move up now from your job as temporary typist to full-time office manager. The trick is to do this without overstepping or making anyone angry. Your procedure: to function now as if the job you want were already yours.

Beginning now, see yourself as you will look and function when you are office manager. How will you dress? What time will you get to work? Without offending, how will you help the girls in the pool to become more efficient?

Carry in your mind the picture of you as office manager, and soon you will dress, look and *be* that manager for all to see, but just to be on the safe side, sign up for an adult education course in personnel management. Never fear, the day that the present manager goes or a new department is opened up, the job you want will be yours. This is the "be" principle. Put to work properly, it never fails. All you have to do to get where you want is to be ready and be seen.

Decide now

You may have wanted to sing long ago and have been wishing that you were good enough to sing in your town's glee club which has a limited membership. Study voice, sing in your church choir or anywhere else you have a chance, dress well when you are in front of an audience, and do work of any kind for the glee club so that you will be in contact. And don't worry. As your voice gets better and better, your invitation will come.

Psychologists I have talked to say this principle works

for club women who want to serve their organization as president, for women who want to get the help of businessmen in raising money for a town project, even for widows who want to get married.

In the notebook you are keeping, write down what you want to be doing a year from today. Then put the "be" principle to work. What you want will come to pass.

PART FIVE

AN EVER-WIDENING CIRCLE OF PEOPLE YOU LIKE TO BE WITH

24

THE SECRET OF MEETING
INTERESTING PEOPLE

There are hostesses who display interesting people to impress and delight their everyday friends, and then the day after a party they forget all about them and go back to their same old circle. Such party givers define as "interesting" anyone who is well known as a writer, politician, artist, entrepreneur, or socialite, and whether such special guests brighten up the table with scintillating talk really doesn't matter. All the hostess wants is for her stars to be there. Her friends can do the talking.

If all you want is to display interesting people, you can find them, but don't expect your life to become more exciting as a result. Your friends will invite you to return parties, perhaps, where they will display their own living set pieces, and that will be the end of that. If empty nest living seems dull now, it will still be dull no matter how good a collector you become, because you will be talking, feeling, thinking, and socializing with the same people as always. To fill your world with people who are interesting to you, you must be interesting to them. There is no deeper secret than that.

Your friends are like your magazines

What four general magazines and one or two newspapers do you and your husband read regularly? Chances are your closest friends read the same ones. There is no more convincing proof that you are attracted to those persons in life whose tastes, ideas, and interests are similar to yours.

If you and your husband subscribe to a special interest magazine that stresses cooking, gardening, hunting and fishing, travel, bridge, hi-fi, sailing, golf, camping, or anything else, you undoubtedly have friends who share this interest. And you are constantly finding new ones.* Because, once again, people who are interested in the same thing are interested in each other. It follows, then, that the primary way to add to your circle of friends is to become genuinely interested in one hobby, project, sport, or cause and go where others congregate who share this same interest.

People to people

There is an organization by the name of People to People at 2401 Grand Avenue, Kansas City, Missouri, which works for around-the-world friendship by encouraging ice skaters far from home to meet other ice skaters, chess players to meet other chess players, artists to get in touch with artists, etc. Should you and your husband be golfers who are

---

* If you like to ski, you can make friends on the slopes; if you like to sail, you will make friends at the dock; if you like to golf, you will make friends on the course; etc.

going to be in Germany, People to People will put you in touch with golfers there. The organization's one-time chairman, Dwight D. Eisenhower, knew from his long-time army experience that a common interest can be a bond between two people wherever they find themselves. If you are planning a trip, write to People to People for the names of others who share your special interest. And, at home, adapt the principle on which this organization is founded.

Obviously, it is absurd to go to the golf course or bridge table to meet interesting people if you don't play either game. You will meet no one. Go where others go who are enjoying themselves doing what *you honestly like to do*. That's where you will make friends. Naturally, the more interests you develop, the more people you will meet who share these interests. Your old friends won't necessarily disappear, but new friends will come, too. When that happens, every day will be more fun than the day before.

Your home is your practice ground

"It seems awfully funny that I can get along with everyone else in the world," an angry wife tells her husband, "but I can't get along with you." Even after twenty-five years of marriage, the lady really believes that she is a peace-loving woman, and that any old or new marriage problem is entirely her husband's fault. *Not true.* If she can't live peacefully in her home with her husband (or with any close friend or relative she happens to be sharing the house with),* she can't have a meaningful relationship with anyone. *Your home tells it like it is; it is your proving ground and your practice place.*

---

* Unless, of course, that person is senile, feeble, hopelessly neurotic, alcoholic, or otherwise disturbed.

Living day by day with a husband helps you to see the world from another's point of view, which is the number one test of maturity. Benjamin DeMott, articulate Amherst professor, says that this is what growth is all about. "A child sees the world from inside of himself. As he lives with people, he becomes aware that the reactions of others are different from his, that they do not feel about everything the way he does, that they do not even see things in the same way. *This awareness is growth.*"

Dealing with differences at home

Practice looking at the world from your husband's point of view, and the quality of your entire life will improve. Let's say, for instance, that you want him to exercise more for his sake but when you suggest a walk at night, he makes some excuse to read instead. One wife in our town, whose husband resisted this way finally found out that walking bored him. So she bought twin bicycles. Then, each night she encouraged her husband to ride to some place, before going to bed. To the mailbox; to return a book; to the corner store to pick up something for breakfast. He saw through her plan, but appreciated the fact that bicycling is faster than walking and liked knowing he was accomplishing something as he got his exercise. Now their nightly ride is a habit.

Maneuvering around a husband's resistance to a suggestion is not usually the answer, say psychologists. Should you want to go to hear an Indian guru, for instance, when your husband thinks Yoga, astrology, or even ESP is far out, go with a matinee-minded friend *and leave him be*. Or if you like Mexican food and your husband does not, serve it to friends when he is away. And if you are always cold and he is always hot, get an electric blanket with a double control and set the dial to where you want it and let him select his own temperature. Make a real effort to see things from his viewpoint.

This does not mean that you must give up your point of view for your husband's way of seeing things. It simply means that you should make an effort to understand how he sees a given situation. In doing so, a solution to a problem can be quickly reached, but better than that, you will be forming the habit of solving all problems in an adult manner which will make life easier for you all along the way.

25

WHY A WELL-ORDERED LIFE IS BOUND TO BRING FRIENDS

Your home is probably immaculate now that there are no children around to mess it up, but it may still be inefficient. Think for a minute. Are you wasting too many steps in a kitchen that was planned for a big family? Are there far too many boxes to wade through under the sink, too many half-used bottles in the bathroom, too much stuff in your drawers? Do you find you spend more and more time looking for things? Time to clear out!

"Clutter makes for a cluttered mind," the founder of a great advertising agency once wrote in a memo to artists, writers, bookkeepers, company officers—all his employees. "Stop now and throw away every unnecessary piece of paper in your office. You will be more creative tomorrow." Autocratic? Some thought so. Sensible? You know it! "Good order," said Edmund Burke, "is the foundation of all good things." Certainly, it is the foundation for a pleasant social life.

Three reasons why order brings friends

1. ORDER TAKES THE BROOM OUT OF YOUR HAND.

A well-groomed home is easier to keep up and gives you more time to think about other activities. "Due to new equipment, today's women whose children are gone comprise the largest leisure class that has ever been known," says Dr. Esther Westervelt, director of the New York State Guidance Center for Women. "So any woman who does needless busy work is covering up for an empty life. No one need go to the supermarket every day, for instance." Lack of clutter gives you extra hours to think about human beings, not housework. This is the first step toward making friends.

2. ORDER PUTS A SMILE ON YOUR FACE.

A well-ordered home makes for graciousness. No need to be rattled when friends stop by if your larder is stocked with easy-to-prepare foods and your bedrooms are ready for guests. And the more sincere your welcome, the more often friends will come.

3. ORDER GETS YOU THERE ON TIME.

Lack of clutter makes for punctuality and other marks of good manners. When you know where things are, you have less last-minute rushing around to keep you from getting to appointments on time. Also, you are always ready to accept a spur-of-the-moment invitation, often the best kind.

Lesson to be learned from Joan Crawford

Joan Crawford, one of the most glamorous actresses of our time and a member of the board of Pepsi-Cola, has a giant clothes closet in her New York duplex which is an effi-

ciency expert's dream. On the padded hanger with every custom-made suit and couture dress and gown is a tag with a
number which matches a number on a box in the closet
which contains the shoes, belt, pin, earrings, gloves, and/
or any other accessories for this particular outfit. Whenever
she travels, she packs the suits, dresses, and gowns in a
wardrobe bag and puts the tagged accessories in envelopes
in a separate case. No hurry-up call to anywhere puts
this beautifully composed woman in a flurry. She's ready!
Start with order and your social life will be as easy as it is
uncomplicated.

26

WHAT IT TAKES TO MAKE A NEW FRIEND EVERY MONTH WITHOUT PUSHING

A common bond between two people is the world's best friendship starter. Think of your personality as a globe on which are planted colored flags indicating your special interests, abilities, and personality traits. If you and your husband, for instance, are big league baseball fans, it stands to reason that a friend of yours with two extra tickets to a world series game will be more apt to invite you than two other friends who don't know a baseball from a hockey puck. If you are someone who knows how to get things done, you will be attractive to the chairman of any committee who respects this ability and sees it in you. If you are witty, you will flag others with a sense of humor who appreciate your way of looking at things. *Like calls to like.*

Think of your five closest friends and of what first attracted you to each one of them and vice versa. If you are an avid bridge player, one of them is probably an equally strong player; if you are from a small town in the Mid-west, another undoubtedly has the same background; if you are active in a church guild, one of your close friends is a member. In the beginning, the gold flag in your personality called to another gold flag; the pink to another; the blue to another. That is the way friendships are made.

Unhappily, when the nest empties, many women suddenly become aware that their old circle of friends has nar-rowed. Old school chums have moved away, business friends have been transferred, a few older friends may have died. When the children were coming in and out with their friends, these changes were not noticed, but now there is a void. Happily, there is also a remedy. Your circle can widen immediately.

One new friend a month

Without being at all forward, you can begin to build one new long-lasting friendship every month wherever you happen to be. Once again, hark to the "be" principle. (1) Develop interests that are a natural result of your abilities and personality; (2) then, be where others can see what you are interested in. Naturally, the deeper your particular interest in anything, the brighter your flag. And never worry that another with the same interest won't be drawn to you—like one human being to another on a desert isle!

As a starter for this month, think of one club activity or event coming up in the future which you know will be en-joyable. This can be a church guild meeting, a regular bridge club or foursome, a monthly fashion luncheon in a local department store, a day of swimming at the beach, skiing at a nearby lodge, a book and author study club meet-ing, a sorority mothers' club meeting, a garden club, any-thing coming up in which you are truly interested.

Now think of one person you have met or seen but do not know well who could share this interest of yours if she knew that it was coming. This time, look for a matching flag in another. Once you sight it, invite the other person to go with you to a coming event that you know will be of interest to both of you.

Look around next Sunday at church for a woman who does not belong to your church guild. Ask her to be your guest at the next meeting. Tell her you will pick her up and take her home. Or, perhaps, your husband has introduced you to the attractively dressed wife of a man with whom he plays golf. Call and ask her to go with you to a fashion show luncheon you are planning to attend.* Or, if one of the homes you pass on your street has a beautiful flower garden, ask the woman who lives there to be your guest at your garden club, or to take part in a local conservation project, or to go with you to a flower show. Call one of your neighbors who plays bridge and ask her to substitute in your regular foursome.

Do not necessarily insist that the person you call be a newcomer in your community. The woman in your church who has never joined your guild may be timid; the attractively dressed friend of your husband may not know about the fashion luncheon; the gardener may be so busy with her flowers she never thinks of what she can contribute to others; and the neighbor who plays bridge may feel that by asking to play she would be pushy. Take the first step toward another with an interest that matches yours. If neither your enthusiasm nor the other's is feigned, you will be on your way to a meaningful friendship.

Forget age

Duplicate bridge players in an important tournament may range in age from twenty to eighty-five, and nobody thinks anything about this for a minute when the play begins. A party at the races may be made up of men and women of all

---

* Never, never, extend such an invitation with the intention of "going Dutch." This is your invitation; you pick up the tab.

ages, and who cares when the horses are off! Canvassers for
your local Community Chest campaign may be far younger
than you or far older, but if you are working with them for a
common cause, you scarcely notice. Once you begin thinking in terms of interest rather than in terms of looks, money,
or social status, age goes overboard. So in your search for
a flag in another that matches one in you, forget age and
other inconsequential circumstances. Look for an unfeigned
interest that is like yours, and friendship will result.

Now—a fascinating new circle-widening game

You may not belong to a club or take part in a community
activity of any kind, and you still can adapt the flag-sighting
principle above and so begin a fascinating, new circle-
widening game. As a first step, write down three solo
activities which you find enjoyable. (Examples: sewing,
swimming, writing, painting, gardening, reading, antique collecting, playing the piano, listening to music.) In the next
week, look in your paper or search out in some other way a
coming exhibit, lecture, show, or concert which appeals to
you because of one of these interests. (Maybe there is a
stitchery exhibit at a local gift shop, a winter swim and luncheon at the "Y," a book and author's luncheon at a department
store, an exhibit of water colors at your library, a lecture on
conservation at a nearby Audubon center, an auction or a
concert at a local college.) Now call someone you have never
spent time with but who you know is interested in the activity you have chosen and ask that person to be your guest
at the coming event. If that person is busy, search out a
second person with this interest and/or a third; it doesn't
matter. Each person you call is going to be complimented by
the fact that you cared enough to see inside her personality
to a true interest she usually indulges in all by herself.

Once you have the first date set, look immediately at your second major interest and for another person (not the same one you're inviting to event number one) who is enthusiastic about this second activity. Invite her to a coming event of interest to both of you and then go to your third major interest. Before you know it, you will have three dates coming up with women you have never been with before. And because of your common bond with each, you can be on your way to making three good friends.

Why this circle-widener works when others fail

Many systems for making friends have been advanced through the years, but all fail when come-on personality tricks and trying to impress others is the suggested basis. Such tricks are superficial. Searching out a particular interest in another person that matches one of your own is something else again. With shared enthusiasm as a bond, a friendship builds from the inside out.

Follow this simple plan and you will make far more than one new friend a month; you will begin a friendship with everyone you meet. Soon, your spare moments will be filled to overflowing with people you really care about. Their enthusiasm will feed your enthusiasm, and vice versa. Your circle will widen by the day, and you will become aware of fascinating new things to do at every turn.

Case history of a widow who wanted to get married

We live on a crooked little two-mile road in Connecticut which hasn't changed much since British sympathizers hid enemy soldiers in Tories' Cave over the hill behind us. Occasionally, a divorced or widowed career woman friend comes up from New York for the weekend. Dressed in slim, stylish pants, she sits in front of our fire and tells us her latest plan to meet men. Next month, golf, even though she hates the game; then, a cruise; pretty soon, bridge lessons "because men play bridge." One woman without a drinking problem told us she joined Alcoholics Anonymous "because so many men belong."

We smile, remembering our pretty Czech friend, Beth, who lived in a tiny house across the road from us and married after a year of widowhood without ever traveling more than three miles to the country store and back.

Beth came to her husband's family farm on our road, she told us, as a bride of seventeen. She lived there for twenty-five years until her husband died and the farm was sold for cash which was distributed to the heirs. She had one child overseas, she was a diabetic and was quiet, lonely, and puzzled when we first met her. Not knowing what to do, she did what she had always done, kept her home sparkling, tended her garden, and baked poppy-seed kolaches and delicate cheesecake which she occasionally sent over for our supper and which melted in our mouths.

Eventually, one day, a sturdy widower came to fix an oil pump, and she offered him a piece of cheesecake and a cup of coffee. The cake, the coffee, the glowing, good-smelling house, the pretty face got to him—three months later she was married.

A few years ago, I told this story on the *Today Show*, and ever since I have been hearing from one widow after another who is learning to make cheesecake. Obviously, there was no point in Beth's trying to be a golfer. Beth did what she could do best; you do what you can do best. Only then will your good points show. When this happens, women and men who are attracted to what you have to offer will seek you out. You will not be alone, and you will be doing what you like to do.

27

MUST YOU TAKE A BACKSEAT WITH YOUR CHILDREN?

A mother is no less a mother when her children leave home, but her role changes, whether they live nearby or far away. She wants the best for her children, but having done everything possible to prepare them for the responsibilities of marriage and parenthood, she is entitled to a release from her old everyday concerns about their welfare. She should not be tempted to tune in daily for the story of what's happening to whom, she must make herself resist for their sakes and hers. And should the children continue to turn to her for old attentions and services, it would be wise for her to reject this dependence, for her sake and theirs.

Not so long ago, few mothers could express relief that the children were through with school and on their own without feeling guilty. This reluctance is giving way, and soon this attitude will be completely passé. The better adjusted the woman, the more she will welcome her freedom, which she will not be ashamed to admit.

Unfortunately, today's grandmothers are in a crossover period. While most have given up the old cookie jar role, many still believe that they must respond to any plea for help from the next generation. Thus, many modern-day mothers of grown children are being used as their mothers were used before them.

What about baby-sitting?

Naturally, you love your grandchildren and enjoy them thoroughly when your children invite you to visit or bring the children to see you. But you won't continue to enjoy them in the same way if you accept every call to baby-sit when another sitter can't be found. Do this and you are allowing yourself to be imposed upon, and, whether you know it or not, you and your son and/or daughter are making a long-term trade.

The mother who is always on tap as a sitter subconsciously expects to be looked after should she ever need help. A mother and daughter, or mother and daughter-in-law, with this kind of unspoken exchange will be dependent on each other and halfway resentful. If you have drifted into such a relationship, break away now.

Time to break the "let's-call-Mother" habit

A graduate mother responds to calls for help from her children for one of three reasons. (1) She has the old-fashioned attitude that it is her job to go on helping her children. (2) Her life is lonely, and she has a subconscious desire to keep up her old dominant role in her children's lives. (3) She wants to be free, but she doesn't know how to say no.

Should you be too involved with your children for any

reason, make a conscious effort to untie the apron strings. Otherwise, you are going to become more and more put upon.

How to escape

One mother told me that she went to work to break her daughter-in-law's let's-get-your-mother-to-take-care-of-the-baby habit. "I like being a receptionist better than being a baby-sitter," she told me, "and the pay is better." Another couple moved into an over-fifty village to discourage their daughter from bringing the children to grandmother's every time she and her husband were going on a vacation. "Here we have a rule that says no children under eighteen, and it's a godsend."

In the long run, the easiest way to put an end to calls to baby-sit (or for money or to listen) is to refuse to get involved. Your children may be surprised the first time you say no, but eventually they will respect your right to live your own life.

"The greatest thing is the world," Montaigne said in the sixteenth century, "is to be self-sufficient," and four hundred years later, few will argue. Maintain your right to be independent and encourage your children to do the same, and you will be saluted. Respond to their every call, and you will end up in the backseat. Far from maintaining your importance to your children, your role will be diminished. In this close family relationship, as in any other, self-reliance gains respect.

You have much to give

The tired woman who allows herself to be thought of as a baby-sitter for her grandchildren has as little to give eventually as any random baby-sitter. But a grandmother with years of patience and wisdom and family tradition to fall back on and pass along can be someone special. So do enjoy your grandchildren, but on your terms.

One thing we have learned: any one of our six grandchildren is an absolute doll if he or she is alone with us. Bring on the pack and everything goes berserk. Another thing: every one of the children behaves better with us than with his or her parents.

This is not due to our superior abilities as disciplinarians. Our effectiveness comes because (1) we have time to give each child complete attention when he visits or travels with us, and (2) we are not acquainted with the little quirks in each one's personality which irritate parents and cause them to overreact. Because we know no better, we expect the best from each child and get it.

What we have to give

Benjamin DeMott tells the story of a wise teacher who encouraged creativity in her small charges each morning. When she came into the classroom she would bring up a problem like this: "The milkman came up on my porch this morning with a lot of big glass bottles of milk. Just as he got to the door, he dropped the bottles, and they all broke, and milk ran all over the porch." As the children sat there thinking about the mess, she would ask, "Now what do you think the milkman did?" Immediately, hands went up as the children told her one after the other what they could see. "The milkman sweeps the porch—Washes it—Picks up the glass—Swears—Apologizes—Borrows the phone to call others waiting for milk"—a hundred different things! As the children described the man's actions and what he said, they were thinking about how *he* felt, taking a giant step toward a more mature outlook.

Our grandchildren in second grade read faster than we did in fifth grade; they do math in a new way that we can't understand; they get facts from television as fast as we get them. In none of these areas can we be of help. But helping them to understand that a brother, sister, playmate, parent, and even a grandparent sees things in a way that is totally different from the way they see it, is one way in which we can contribute. It is in small ways like this that we can be of help, we believe. Certainly, we have a lot of fun trying.

Comfort and respect

When our children come to our house with their children, they can now stay in their own "suite" complete with its little refrigerator and pullman kitchen, so they are comfortable—and so are we.

When we go to their house, we achieve this same comfort for both them and us by staying near them (not with them) in an inn or motel. Just as they have breakfast and baths in their quarters at our house, we do the same when we visit them. And at neither house do my daughters and I work together in the kitchen. I get the dinner at my house; they do the same at their house. They respect my way of doing things, and I respect their way.

There is an old proverb: "He that respects not is not respected." Respect your children and grandchildren, and you will be respected in return. Once you achieve this respect, you won't ever be relegated to a backseat in life. And you won't be waiting around for letters from your children, either. Your life will be so full, your children will be waiting for yours!

PART SIX

LOOKING AT THE WORLD WITH A "SEEING EYE" WHEREVER YOU HAPPEN TO BE

28

TRAINING YOURSELF TO
SEE BEYOND THE OBVIOUS

You know that you do not react to or feel about everything the same way as others, but have you ever stopped to consider that no other person sees what is right in front of his eyes the same way that you do? Your way of perceiving everything around you is unique.

"Great photographers live by their eyes," Victor Keppler, director of Westport's Famous Photographers School, told me one day. "The camera is simply the tool that liberates their ability to see what others miss." By *seeing,* Victor Keppler doesn't mean seeing *details* that others miss; quite the opposite. He means seeing an *idea* that others cannot see.

In 1936, *Life* magazine sent Alfred Eisenstaedt to Ethiopia to record the plight of a primitive, poorly equipped army in its fight against fascist Italy's tanks, planes, and bombs. His picture (taken from behind) of the cracked, mud-caked bare feet of a prone Ethiopian soldier instantly communicated the essence of the struggle. This is what is meant by *seeing beyond the obvious.*

Recording what you see with a camera is a good way to develop your unique seeing experience. For unless some meaning is conveyed by a photograph, its reason for being is sterile. One day, the great portrait photographer, Philippe Halsman, was shooting the Duke and Duchess of Windsor and was saddened to notice that his subjects looked tense, tired, and old. Knowing instinctively that good portraiture is good psychology, he said softly, "Remember, in the eyes of the world, you are the most romantic couple of this century." Instantly, the Duke and Duchess smiled, relaxed, and looked ten years younger, and the camera captured their love story.

Take a camera when you travel

Take a camera with you on a trip to record what you see that others miss, and you will have an unforgettable time. With this approach, you will not stand with your husband in front of St. Mark's and ask a passerby to click the shutter of your camera to show the folks back home that you were in Venice. You will record what was interesting to you. Maybe this will be your own evidence that Venetian palaces are sinking into the sea. Or it will be a close-up of Venetian lace that reveals the difference between real and machine-made lace. Or it may be a picture of a Murano glassblower who is molding a decorative effect into a vase as he blows, something you didn't know before could be done.

Anytime you become interested enough in something to ask a question, take a picture of what you learn. "Is Venice really sinking?" Take a picture as the guide tells you where the water level was when he was a boy. Or find your own truth. Your pictures will be exciting, and you will have a better time.

Developing the courage to comment

The photographer (or painter) who simply records the reality of what is in front of him is not an artist. Art comes in when a comment is made. Once you know that you see things in a special way, find ways to comment with camera, canvas, or letters on what you see that others miss. Any talent you have will grow as your personal viewpoint begins to emerge in everything you do, and your life will be far more enjoyable wherever you may be.

29

WHY A REPORTER'S APPROACH TO TRAVEL MAKES FOR A POSITIVE ATTITUDE

A great reporter covering a battle in Vietnam, an investiture in Wales, or an accident at Chappaquiddick needs no camera to record his experience. He has trained his eyes to see, his ears to hear, and his mind to remember. Like an expert photographer, he prunes away details to get to the essence of a story as he sees and feels it.

Ask such a reporter afterward what airline he used, if he liked where he stayed, and if the food was good, and he will be bored. Yes, he traveled, slept, and ate, but none of this had anything to do with why he was traveling. He was where he was to learn what he could learn. Adopt such an attitude when you travel, and you will never be bored again.

Three trips we will never forget

A few years ago, my husband and I collaborated* on three science books for children: *What Does the Tide Do?*, *What Does the Sun Do?*, and *What Does the Cloud Do?* For the first, Cle made his sketches along the coast at Martha's Vineyard, and we researched our oceanographic facts at Woods Hole; for our second, he sketched on the desert near Phoenix, and we did our research at the Fort Apache Indian Reservation; for the third, he photographed clouds through the glass dome of a train headed toward the state of Washington, and we did our research with the help of rangers on Mount Rainier. Did we have any discomfort on any of these trips? I can't remember. Did we have a good time? Never better. Today, when we travel, we do advance research before each stop and are as deeply interested in everything we see as we were then. Naturally, we get ten times the enjoyment from our trips now than in the old days when we traveled simply "to get away."

Three specific ways to deepen your enjoyment while traveling

1. Start out with a specific place, experience, or high spot in mind. Don't go to a place just because everyone is going there. Go to France to tour the wine country; Florence, to see the work of Renaissance painters; Minneapolis or Atlanta for Opera Week. Go to New York to see the new Broadway plays; to Mexico to buy Spanish things for that room you're doing over.

* Cle did the art; I did the writing.

2. Do advance research on what you are going to see* and where you are going to see it. Go to your local librarian for books about both. (Before going to Minneapolis for Opera Week, know the performers and the story of the operas you will hear. Find out what else is going on so that you can arrange to see the Guthrie Theater, the Walker Art Center, the General Mills and/or Pillsbury kitchens.)

3. Give yourself extra time going and coming for side trips, shopping expeditions, and visits with friends.

With a specific destination in mind and a reporter's attitude toward this, you will approach every trip you take with a positive attitude. Any little discourtesies or discomforts along the way will be objectively noted, and your travels will take on a new dimension they never had before.

---

* If the high spot of your husband's trip is a world series game, know the participating teams and players, or don't go.

30

TWELVE PLACES TO GO NEAR HOME WHERE YOU HAVE NEVER BEEN BEFORE

Annabel Irving, a slim, attractive widow who owns and runs a beautifully cared-for five-hundred-acre farm near us, has a herd of Black Angus which recently produced the Grand Champion Steer at the Eastern States Exposition in Springfield, Massachusetts. By far the busiest person we know in northwest Connecticut, she is also the most stimulating hostess. Day or weekend guests at Iron Mountain Farm talk for months afterward about their memorable walks or drives to nearby places arranged by their hostess with their interests in mind. Only recently have we come to know Mrs. Irving's way of keeping up on things, which is a system any woman anywhere can adapt.

A complete file of interesting places to go

In a compact one-drawer file labeled "Places to Go," Mrs. Irving has seventy-five or a hundred folders sectioned off into compartments: Art Galleries and Exhibits, Historical Places, Museums, Music, Movies, Nature Trips, Picnic Places, Special Events, Theatres, Walking Trips, etc. Each folder in each compartment contains brochures, newspaper articles, and magazine clippings about a given place and a schedule of hours and days when this gallery, museum, or park is open.

Should she have five or six friends for the weekend who like to walk, she may suggest at Saturday breakfast that they go over the fields two or three miles to a pit and blast furnace where iron was once mined, or she may drive them to the Sharon Audubon Center for a conducted tour around a pond by a trained ecologist or to our Squash Hollow Road in New Milford for a three-mile walk past Tories' Cave along the Blue Spur of the Appalachian Trail that cups our land. For music lovers, she suggests an afternoon concert at Music Mountain in Canaan or a summer concert by the Boston Symphony at Tanglewood across the border in Lenox, Massachusetts. For history buffs, she recommends a drive to see the handsome old homes and America's first law school at Litchfield, or to Mark Twain's house, next door to Harriet Beecher Stowe's house, in Hartford. When she has a houseful for the weekend (or a cow about to drop a calf), Mrs. Irving may not go with the party but she always has every detail of their drive or walk worked out to perfection, and she is always waiting at dinner for news of what happened. No wonder her guests look forward with delight to an invitation from Iron Mountain Farm.

Six easy rules for your personal use

What Mrs. Irving does for her guests you can do wherever you live for your own enjoyment and that of your husband and friends. The six steps below will get you started.

1. Buy a simple one-drawer file cabinet and fifty file folders.
2. Go to your library and look up places of interest within a fifty-mile radius of your home.* Make notes and file.
3. Write to the Development Commission in your State House (and to the same commission in states bordering yours) and ask for folders that list historical sites and/or recreation spots.
4. Clip and file any stories you come across about nearby places.
5. Join your local historical society and read and talk to curators and librarians about the history of your state.
6. Pick up road maps and guides (with notes about places of interest) at AAA, your local gas station, and nearby tourist stations.

One all-day trip a month for a year

Let's say that you live in Marshalltown, Iowa, and for some reason you have never been up to the northeast part of the state. So you set aside one Saturday in the fall when the maple leaves are turning, and ask your husband to drive you and two of your friends he enjoys to Decorah (located near towering spires of limestone along the Iowa River) to see the Norwegian American Historical Museum, log schoolhouse, and furnished American pioneer houses on the campus of Luther College. On the way home you stop to see

---

* Excellent sources: *American Heritage New Pictorial Encyclopedic Guide to the United States,* 16 Vols., New York, Dell Publishing Co., Inc., 1965; *Mobil Travel Guide to . . .* (for each section of the country), New York, Simon and Schuster, 1966; *A Guide to Your State's Roads, Lore and People,* compiled by the Federal Writers' Project, Boston, Houghton Mifflin Company, 1938.

the Antonín Dvořák Memorial at Spillville, where the composer created part of his "New World" Symphony, the elaborately carved Bily clocks in the home where Dvořák lived, and the world's tiniest church, the St. Anthony of Padua Chapel at Festina.

After this good day, plan another Saturday's outing for next month, southeast this time, to the religiously motivated 250-year-old German settlement of seven villages known as the Amana colonies or west to the library on Morrill Road at Ames to see the Grant Wood murals, among the Iowa artist's best.

Each month of the year take a new trip, plan long drives and picnics for the summer, short trips to indoor places in the winter. Your only rules: (1) go each time to a town with stops that are new to all in your car; (2) invite two friends to share each trip (preferably, a different twosome every time); (3) don't repeat. Take twelve once-a-month trips in your own state; then go over the border to a nearby state for short trips during the next year. Make notes as you travel, and bring home brochures and maps so that you can tell newcomers to the state and guests passing through about places at which to stop.

One glamour weekend a year

One summer Saturday, my husband surprised me by chartering a plane in Danbury to take one of our grandchildren and me to Boston. At the Boston airport, friends met us with their grandchild and took us for a drive along well-marked Freedom Trail past the Old South Meeting House where the Boston Tea Party was plotted, the Old State House where the Declaration of Independence was read from the balcony in 1776, Paul Revere's house, and the Old North Church. After some unforgettable lobster, we went to the

Hatch Shell on the Charles River for a Boston "pops" concert. That night, we stayed in a pleasant hotel, with a swimming pool on an upper level, where we swam early Sunday before visiting the Christian Science Mother Church, Bunker Hill monument, and *Old Ironsides,* which is berthed in the Boston Navy Yard. The airport was clouded over, so we rented a car and drove late that day to Connecticut. Total time away: two days and one night. Total cost: not much more than an overnight trip to New York to take friends to dinner and the theater. But we remember that whirlwind trip more than we do many of our month-long vacations.

Make plans for at least one overnight trip in your year as well as eleven trips to nearby places, and for this one trip, go heavy on the glamour. In Virginia, go for a Saturday and Sunday to magnificently restored Williamsburg or drive to Mr. Jefferson's wonderful Monticello on top of its "little mountain" in Charlottesville, or fly to West Virginia's Greenbrier at White Sulphur Springs for a weekend of golf, riding, or swimming. A trip does not have to be long to be memorable, but it does have to be well-planned.

Don't push for a lollapalooza weekend until your husband has gone away with you for a few easy one-day trips first. Then you probably won't have to push. He will be as enthusiastic as you about setting out with a happy companion to explore this country he has never stopped to think much about.

Do not disturb

As you plan your first year's trips with your husband, *absolutely refuse to let minor interruptions get in your way.* Stay home for a party one time, a surprise drop-in from the children on another, and a hurry-up committee meeting on a third, and your project will never take off. Go once, twice, three times and your project will gather momentum along with a force of its own.

In the beginning, your husband will not be as serious as you about your little trips, but when he realizes how much these days with him mean to you, he will be pleased and soon will help you all he can. The calls on his time, however, may be more demanding than on yours, so do not show your disappointment when he has to change days. Adjust *immediately* but *specifically*. Write down on your calendar another day that is right for both of you. The main thing: *keep going*.

Decide what is important

Suppose you and your husband are about to set off on your first well-planned all-day trip, and along comes a special delivery from a long-forgotten friend, cousin, or business acquaintance who will be arriving in your town late that night and wants to stay with you. Will you cancel your plans with your husband to wait for someone you haven't seen for years and who may not arrive until after you could be home from your trip anyway?

Suggestion: Leave the lights on in the house and leave a note on the door telling your visitor that the key is next door, should he arrive before you get home. Then, ask your neighbor to do you the favor of letting your guest in the house. Naturally, you will have flowers and a great big welcome note in the room where he or she will be staying, which will explain that you will be home late and will see him in the morning.

This way, you will be a thoughtful absentee hostess in case your guest arrives before you get back, but you won't be robbing yourself and your husband of a lovely day. Stay home, and you will be breaking a date with your husband

and setting a precedent that will get in the way of your entire plan from then on. One way, life will be riding you; the other, you will be riding life.

Quick action is sign of youth

If he's in business, your husband may have to take off for a trip on an afternoon's notice. When he senses that you are flexible and that you love traveling with him, he will begin to ask you to go along. Cancel anything that you can cancel—and go. Spur of the moment thinking is a youthful sign—and quick trips are great!

You won't always have time before take-offs to bone up on what you are going to see, but you can always keep your mind and your eyes open once you get to where you are going. "A book that is shut," says an old proverb, "is but a block." And an unlooked-at painting, church, or town are nothing more than blobs of oil, a pile of stone, or a bunch of houses. Open your mind and eyes when you travel, and every trip will be a joy whether you are far away or just off for the day to some place new in your own or a nearby state.

31

YOUR CHOICE OF NINE EXCURSIONS THAT TAKE ONLY FIVE DAYS AWAY FROM WORK

If you and your husband are both still working, dovetailing your annual vacation time to get away for a three-week holiday may be out of the question every year. But with a little advance planning you should be able to take five (or preferably six) days off together once or twice a year for a quick trip to a far-away place that would have been impossible when your children were at home.

Airlines, resorts, hotels, and tourist bureaus are coming up each season with fascinating excursion plans for just such couples as you. *So dream a little*. Tonight, take a look at the terrific travel possibilities that are now available to you.

No Chicago bottleneck

If you live in St. Louis, Denver, or Kansas City, there is no stopover in Chicago anymore on the way east. And the same holds true if you are traveling to the West Coast from Cleveland, Philadelphia, or another large city in the East. The old Chicago time-waster is no more.

Two ways to travel by air at a reduced rate

For this first air-travel project we will assume that you live west of the Mississippi in a city (or near a city) with a jet-serviced airport.*

If you can be away for seven days or more and do not have to travel by air on Friday afternoon or on Monday morning, you can save money by traveling as a couple on a family plan or as an individual (or two individuals) on a Discover America excursion, which is even less expensive.†

Five trips that begin at the airport

Let's say that you have managed to get five days off in one week and Monday off in the following. Where can you go from Kansas City on your Discover America plan? Here are five suggestions:

1. To New York on a Saturday morning—and away in the afternoon by boat to Nassau or Bermuda. Usually this trip calls for two days on the boat going, two days there, and two days on the boat back to New York thus arriving by Saturday. That leaves a weekend for theatre and museum trips in New York before flying home Monday afternoon.

2. To Portland, Maine, on Casco Bay on Saturday, where you can begin a week's sail (or drive to Boothbay Harbor or

* You can plan your trips as easily if you live on either coast or east of the Mississippi; you simply parallel the specific examples given here.
† Usually, on a family plan, the husband pays full fare, and his wife pays 25 percent to 50 percent less. On the present Discover America excursion plan, both fares are reduced. Advantage of family plan: Your reduction applies when you travel first class; Discover America excursion plan applies to coach fare only.

to Rockland on Penobscot Bay to begin your sail) on an old windjammer, refitted to give comfort. Sail along the scenic Maine coast, stopping to explore a few of the hundreds of fascinating islands that dot the sea. Great for fishing!

3. To Alaska for a week of riding on a dude ranch near Fairbanks. On the way back, stop on Saturday and Sunday in Seattle, and take a short side hop to Victoria for the day or go for a drive to the glacier-hung Olympic Mountains along the coast and come back through the rain forests.

4. Fly to Jackson, Mississippi, in March and rent a car. Drive to Vicksburg for a day at the Museum on the old *Stern-wheeler* moored at China Street; then on to Natchez for the annual pilgrimage of magnificent antebellum homes. Go down to Biloxi and to the Bay of St. Louis (the praline capital of the world) for some fishing before heading home.

5. Fly to Boise, Idaho, and rent a car, and drive through Ketchum, where Hemingway lived, to ski for a week at Sun Valley. Or drive in July to Mt. Borah, Idaho's tallest peak, near Mackay, and then go up north to the Salmon River and drive through the canyons along spectacular Route 93.

Four trips by land

1. Drive to Sun City, north of Phoenix, where you can stay in an immaculate, beautifully furnished "apartment" for just $75 a week as you look at model homes and consider the possibility of buying a place in this village for over-fifty residents. No need to buy just because you take advantage of the promotion. Sun City's management knows that you will go home and tell others about your stay, and that's promotion enough.*

---

* Apartments are much in demand and have to be spoken for long in advance. For full details write to: Del Webb Corp., P.O. Box 555, Sun City, Arizona 85351.

2. In the fall drive to Chicago, stopping on the way for a day in Springfield to see the only house that Lincoln ever owned, the courthouse where he delivered his "House Divided" speech, and the tomb where he is buried. In Chicago, see the Art Museum and Field Museum, the Aquarium, and the season's new plays. On the way home stop for a football game at the University of Illinois in Urbana.

3. Take an unforgettable train trip to the West Coast on the Santa Fe (along the old Santa Fe Trail and eventually past the Nixon home at San Clemente). Or go to Minneapolis and then by Northern Pacific to Portland, stopping at Billings for an overnight trip (by rented car) into Yellowstone Park. Go up to Seattle or down to Los Angeles and back.* A guide in the Vista Dome car will tell you what you're passing.

4. If you are a history buff, antique collector, or jazz buff, drive to New Orleans in the pre-Lenten Mardi Gras season or afterward. Poke around in the French quarter, eat at Antoine's and other famous restaurants, take a thirty-mile boat trip through Louisiana's bayou country, and listen to old-time jazz. Stay, if you can, in a delightful hotel just off the Court of the Three Sisters called Maison de Ville. Morning coffee in the garden is worth what you pay—and if you like to swim, you can make arrangements to go for lunch and a swim at one of the large hotels nearby.

One out-of-the-country trip every two years

You have a glamorous and not too expensive life in the making if you plan eleven one-day trips (and one glamour weekend) a year to some place new in your state, plus one

---

* Jo Esposito, our travel agent at Robustelli Travel Service in Danbury, tells us that Union Pacific has marvelous one-week tours that you can book direct or through your travel agent.

or two week-long Discover America trips out of your state.

To round out your travel plans, take one long trip out of the country every two or three years. Do not disdain tours. Fly to a selected list of European museums in a chartered plane full of travelers interested in art, or go on a cruise to the Mediterranean on a ship chartered by a local club, or fly with friends on a chartered plane to the Greek Isles. You save money by going with a group, learn new facts about a subject in which you have a particular interest, and travel with compatible friends who share your interest.

Expect the best when you travel, but know, too, that you will have frequent surprises. Keep going, anyway, the discomfort will pass.

Lesson learned from Robert Frost

On his seventy-fifth birthday, Robert Frost was asked what was the most important truth he had learned about life that he could pass along. "I can answer in three words," said the wise New England poet, "it goes on." No lesson you learn from this book or any other will stand you in such good stead, especially when you're traveling. Life is bound to startle you occasionally when you're on the move, but don't stay home just because you anticipate occasional upsets. *Ride out the storm*.

Story of a hurricane and a wedding

The E. S. Andersons of Gulfport, Mississippi, raised their four children in a great house anchored to the rim of the Gulf of Mexico with thick cypress timbers which resisted all gales until Hurricane Camille. Then, just five days before his last child's wedding and with a travel folder in his pocket describing a surprise trip he had in mind for his wife, Andy Anderson, fifty-seven, saw his house and all its furnishings (including Margie's wedding presents) swept away by the wind.

"We are going ahead with the wedding," he told the town the next day. "It represents a spirit of resolve to us, a belief in life." Four days later, he escorted his daughter down the dank, muddy aisle of the Methodist Church into the arms of her new husband, and then turned to his wife and asked her if she thought they were going to be able to find enough to do in their empty nest.

Few couples have as giant an upset or as drastic a test of determination as the Andersons, but all bump into surprises as they plan together. Don't let upsets throw you, or you will do nothing. Keep moving along, and when a plan is interrupted, make a new one and go on. *Ride life: don't let life ride you.* Make this your rule and each day will be an adventure wherever you find yourself.

32

HOW TO TRAVEL AROUND
THE WORLD WITHOUT
LEAVING HOME

We have parents and aunts in their eighties who do not take strenuous trips with many stops anymore or do any skiing, surfing, or deep-sea diving; yet, without leaving their comfortable homes, they go everywhere. "Through Tom," one of them wrote after a recent visit from our oceanographer son, "we went spelunking this week along the coast of Jamaica."

In the last year, our family's octogenarians have watched the sun in northern Alaska go down and come up without going out of sight via slides from our Army engineer son-in-law, learned through letters from our art historian daughter-in-law how frescoes were peeled away from Italian walls and transported to the Metropolitan Museum in New York, sailed on an old-time whaling vessel out of Mystic, Connecticut, with my husband and my grandson who kept a log.

"How do you get the children," someone asked us, "to write and visit their grandparents so often?" We never ask the children to go to see their older relatives; they want to go because in the homes of their grandparents, they find an intelligent audience honestly interested in their adventures which many of their own age are too busy to enjoy. The key again: *unfeigned interest.*

A unique club that anyone can form

Twenty-five years ago, Fredric March, the actor, Fred Redefer, renowned professor at New York University, Monroe Goldwater, New York lawyer, and Dr. Burrill Crohn, one of Eisenhower's doctors and the discoverer of Crohn's disease, organized a unique club which still meets at nine o'clock on Saturday night during the summer, in its own clubhouse in the rural Merryall section near New Milford, Connecticut. Its members (limited to 250 because that's all the clubhouse, once an old grange hall, will hold) come to hear an hour's talk by a member, town resident, or visitor on any subject that that year's program director feels will interest the audience. One Saturday night Jack and Elie Leon, long-time members, showed close-up pictures of wild animals taken on a safari in Africa with Freddie and Florence March. On another Saturday night, our neighbor, Norman Flayderman, world authority on scrimshaw, showed examples from his collection of carvings on whalebone and told the history of this American folk art. And on still another Saturday night, Letitia Baldrige, in town to visit her brother who is president of Scovill Manufacturing, talked to members about experiences she had in Paris, Rome, and Washington, where she served at various times as social secretary to Ambassador and Mrs. Bruce, Clare Boothe Luce, and the John F. Kennedys.

What we do at Merryall, you can do anywhere.* Our dues (fifteen dollars a year) cover building maintenance; our

---

* No formal clubhouse is needed. Members can meet in a church or in any adequate building that is free for the evening.

speakers and musical programs are either given gratis by members and/or friends of members, or a particular performance is paid for out of the goodness of one member's heart. The only criterion for membership: *are you interested?* If the answer is yes, members know that suggestions for programs will be stimulating and each week's audience will be big and enthusiastic.

A few members at Merryall travel constantly; others never leave home. But all are interested in what is going on in the world. Make this a characteristic of your personality and/or your club, and all the "Big-Time Doers" you know will beat a path to your door.

PART SEVEN

NO FINAL RETIREMENT PLAN EVER!

33

COMING UP: THE COMFORTABLE LIFE THAT EVERYONE WANTS

If you are like most adult Americans, rich or poor, living an urban or a rural life, your number-one goal is a comfortable retirement. And unless you are exceptionally efficient or are at the top of the nation's affluent, you probably do not feel that you now have the money and/or the plan you need for lifetime security. In a recent opinion research poll, conducted by Louis Harris and Associates, Inc., for *Life* magazine, adult men and women were given a list that included such everyday wants as owning a color TV set, steak and roast beef whenever you want, and a house of your own. When each person interviewed was asked, "What do you want money for?" about 70 percent of those who read the list selected "comfortable retirement" as what they wanted most but did not have. Even women who were relatively young said they wanted a "comfortable retirement" far more than to "go out for entertainment once a week," to "take a trip across the country," or even to "put all their children through college."

As empty nesters in your forties or fifties, you and your husband will be far happier if you determine what a comfortable retirement means to you and if you get rid of any vague apprehension about not being able to achieve it. The money section earlier in the book should have erased your major financial fears, but here are three more security-insuring steps to take as you look ahead: (1) Decide where, how, and when you will have your comfortable retirement. (2) Decide what you must do to achieve this ideal life. (3) Consider several alternate plans for a comfortable retirement no matter what happens.

Two basic ingredients in your recipe for retirement

Every person's recipe is different for happiness in retirement, but one thing is sure. There can be no ideal life for anyone over sixty-five (or younger, for that matter) that does not include two basic ingredients besides money: physical comfort, and psychological comfort. The degree to which you incorporate these two needs into your recipe for the future depends less on the size of your bank account than on your ability to face up to the way life is now and is apt to be tomorrow.

INGREDIENT NUMBER ONE: PHYSICAL COMFORT

As noted before, your daily physical comfort (and that of your husband) is dependent on your living in a climate that is right for your body chemistry (and his). To live out your life in a climate that intensifies any tendency you may have to arthritis, rheumatism, or bronchial trouble or exaggerates any allergic reactions is just plain silly. Because of business commitments you may not be able to leave the uncomfortable climate you live in now, but you certainly can make plans to live elsewhere in retirement, and this should be your goal.

Your aim should also include a home that is comfortable now and will be later. You have already taken a straight look at your present home's size, arrangement, and furnishings. Now ask yourself if this home is always going to be as right for you as it is now, as easy to keep up inside and out. If the answer is no, begin making simple purchases and modifications that will make life easier later, which means your home will also be easier to live in now. And if simple modifications will never produce long-term comfort, move as soon as possible. Even if your answer is yes, there are two more questions to ask yourself.

If necessary, can I (or can my husband) live here alone as comfortably as either of us can live anywhere else? And, do we have enough health and hospital insurance to take care of either or both of us here or in surroundings that will be physically comfortable, no matter what happens?

If the answer to the first question is no, decide what alternate moves are practical and possible in case of emergency. And if the answer to the second question is no, rework your financial planning to include more hospitalization. With these few considerations settled, your lifetime comfort (and, remember, your physical comfort is all we are talking about here) is assured.

INGREDIENT NUMBER TWO: PSYCHOLOGICAL COMFORT

A sixty-five-year-old woman near us who was recently widowed has an estate consisting largely of a big hard-to-keep-up home and forty rolling acres of gardens and flowers and pools. She can be sure of a lifetime of physical comfort if she sells the big place where she lived with her husband, rents a small apartment on the green, insures herself against any eventuality, and lives on what she takes in from social security and the return from her invested capital. But the prospect makes her psychologically uncomfortable.

"I love flowers and water and grass," she told us last month, "and I will work harder to live in the country." So now she's deciding which of these three courses to take: (1) She can sell thirty acres of land, rent her home furnished on its ten acres, and for one year sublet a furnished condominium in a residential development nearby which will provide her with flowers and grass and waterfalls without the responsibilities of maintenance. If she enjoys condominium living after "trying it on," she can sell her big house at the end of the year and buy a condominium. (2) She can sell thirty acres and use the capital to convert her home into three apartments. In this way she will have an income from two apartments, an appreciating investment in her home and the remaining ten acres, far less space in the house to take care of, and the joy of working in her own gardens on her own land. (3) She can add to her income by renting two bedrooms in her home to school teachers for the winter and sell nothing for a year. During this time her land and home will be appreciating and she will have time to consider still other places and plans. In her case, the psychological comfort she feels in the country far outweighs any lack of physical comfort this kind of life entails.

When considering a dramatically different move for reasons of physical comfort, ask yourself these questions: (1) Will this new, more comfortable environment give me psychological comfort as well as physical comfort? (2) Will I be making this move because I truly prefer this new way of life (and *not* because of another's preference or recommendation)? (3) Is there an alternate move possible for me (without too much expense) if this one does not work out the way I think it will?

Answer yes to these three queries, and you will be happy in the move you are contemplating. Answer no, and you have some more thinking to do. You can't be comfortable in a psychological environment that doesn't fit you any more than you can be happy in a climate that makes you physically uncomfortable!

34

CAN YOU ALWAYS LIVE
AS WELL AS NOW...
NO MATTER WHAT?

With the help of the simple charts in this chapter, you can figure what you spend (and what more you will have to spend if prices go up) to maintain your present standard of living. Also, you can see at a glance what income you can count on after sixty-five.

Everytime you read about inflated prices, mounting taxes, and increased life expectancy you may wonder if you will have enough to live well in later years when you may not have as large an income as now. The answer is simple. If what you can count on dips no lower in your chart than your anticipated expenses, you have nothing to worry about. If your expenses to live as you want to live add up to more than what you will be taking in, you can do something about this in advance. Either way, you will have nothing to worry about.

Common worries of empty nesters

"What if my husband doesn't keep his present job until retirement?" you may be wondering. "What if one of us gets sick and we use up all our savings?" "How can we possibly live like this when we're over sixty-five and taking in half what we're making now?"

To begin with, determine with the help of the chart on page 224 what your basic annual expenses will have to be five years from now to maintain your present standard of living. Simply put down what you now spend for a given need, plus any additional percentage as specified.

ANNUAL EXPENSES—FIVE YEARS FROM NOW

Mortgage payments (same as now—unless your home will then be paid for) or rent (Figure 10 percent more for rent.) _____

Home maintenance and insurance (Add 10 percent for present cost.) _____

Property taxes (Add 15 percent to present cost.) _____

Food for two (Add 10 percent to what it now costs for you to eat all meals at home.) _____

Medical care, health and accident insurance (Add 20 percent to what you are spending unless you will be over sixty-five in five years and entitled to Medicare.*) _____

Clothing and personal needs (Figure that you can get along as well on one-half of what you now spend if your husband buys one good suit instead of two and you buy one good dress instead of two.) _____

Transportation (same as what you now spend for purchase and upkeep of one car) _____

Vacations (Figure twice what you are now spending. You will want to travel more, not less, as work time lessens.) _____

Gifts (Figure one-third more than you now spend. You will want to give costlier gifts to your children and grandchildren when they live far from home.) _____

Entertainment (approximately 10 percent of your food-for-two figure) _____

TOTAL AMOUNT NEEDED FIVE YEARS FROM NOW TO MAINTAIN PRESENT LIVING STANDARD _____

Now add 10 percent on top of this for savings and investments. _____

TOTAL NEEDED _____

If you will be under sixty-five, chances are that your present income is greater than the amount you will have to spend five years from now to live as well as you now do. So ask yourself these questions: (1) How much of our excess income can we now invest to rid ourselves of that nagging

---

* Today, Medicare pays:
  • For the first sixty days in the hospital—all but the first $52.
  • For the sixty-first through the ninetieth day in the hospital—all but $13 a day.
  • For lifetime reserve days used—all but $26 a day.
  • For the twenty-first through the hundredth day in an extended-care facility—all but $6.50 a day.

"What if" question?* (2) Can we live on a reduced income five years from now without sacrificing quality in our lifestyle? (3) Between us, can we manage to take in as much as we need to live as we do today?

When you get to retirement age

To maintain your present standard of living in retirement, you will have to take in at least as much then as you now pay out for basic expenses, eliminating mortgage payments, of course, should your home be paid for by that time. In determining your future income, you will need to know what Social Security benefits you will be entitled to when you reach sixty-five,† as things now stand.

After sixty-five, if you earn no more than $1,680 a year from work you do,‡ you will be entitled to full benefits (and even if you earn more, you will be entitled to some benefits). The amount of your benefits will depend on what your husband and/or you have paid into social security through the years.

What to count on after sixty-five

Whether you are forty-four, fifty-four, or sixty-four, write down on the next page what you can count on for your livelihood after sixty-five if all goes well.

---

* The chart shows 10 percent for savings. For maximum security, you can aim for 25 percent.

† Type your husband's Social Security number and name and address on a government card (and yours, if you work, on another) and send to Social Security Administrations, P. O. Box 57, Baltimore 3, Maryland. Ask for the total amount credited to this account. Take one or both statements to your local Social Security office (usually in your post office) and ask the counselor to what benefits you will be entitled.

‡ After age seventy-two, you will receive full Social Security benefits no matter how much you earn per year.

Monthly Social Security check (for husband)	_____
Monthly Social Security check (for wife)	_____
Monthly income from one or two company pensions	_____
Monthly income from annuity	_____
Monthly income from real estate holdings	_____
Approximate monthly income from stocks and bonds	_____
Monthly income from trust or inheritance	_____
Income of husband (not to exceed $1,680 annually)*	_____
Income of wife (not to exceed $1,680 annually)*	_____
Total annual income after retirement	_____

To size up how this annual income will compare with what you are now making, write down your present annual income.   _____

If you are now making $35,000 a year, and, after sixty-five, you can count on only $15,000 (or are making $8,500 and can count on only $4,500), the quality of your life will not be diminished if your new $15,000 or $4,500 income covers your present basic expenses. That is the bench mark.

Save and you're home free

Income after sixty-five that comes from interest, dividends, rentals from real estate, pensions, insurance policy benefits for disability or accident does not count as money earned. Thus, the more you save, the more *free* money (in addition

---

* Case in point: A man of sixty-six can count on drawing full Social Security benefits of $160.50 a month, and his wife can count on drawing from his earnings, $80.30 a month. In addition, he may have a job lined up to do the bookkeeping for a local electrical shop for $140 a month, and she may be taking in the same amount for helping out in the library of a nearby private school. Their total monthly income then, besides any income from savings, will be $520.80.

to Social Security benefits) you will have to spend later on. Should your anticipated retirement income be less than your basic annual expenditures, cut back to a smaller home now that the children are gone, and the sooner the better. With what you make from the sale of your home and what you can save in one year, you can furnish your home exquisitely. Thus, you will live with no feeling of lack before retirement, will save easily until retirement, and will have no worries afterward.

What do you owe your children?

You owe them nothing, but there is one kindness you can do for them and that is to protect yourself from the possibility of eventual dependency. (If it comes, cope, but for both their sake and yours try to avoid this.) The children owe you the same consideration. Other than that, your lives and the financial affairs of both should be separate.

Your children would not be human if they did not consider what inheritance may be coming from you. So tell them, if you want to, but don't stint in your own life to help them build a more comfortable life. Build this life for *you*.

What about gifts?

When your children are away and you sense their needs and see their plans and aims, you are going to be tempted to help them all you can.* If you can afford this, fine; if not,

* Remembered from speech on wills by Suzanne Powers, lawyer in Bethel, Connecticut: "You can give any child three thousand dollars in any year (over a period of years, if you want) without your paying a gift tax and without his paying any income tax on this amount."

don't sacrifice. They will earn as you earned, and, anyway, they won't remember that you gave them the money to have the garage extended, so you won't be a hero, if that's what you're thinking.

You can be a hero, however, by giving totally unexpected gifts. We have a foolproof pleasure-giver that we give as a surprise to our six children, four children-in-law, and six grandchildren every Christmas. We give a community gift of land.

A few years ago, we figured that we were spending an average of $40 per person for our sixteen children and grandchildren every Christmas, and that no one was remembering much one year what we gave the last. So we switched.

Each year, we begin in January to look for a large parcel of undeveloped land; then, at Christmas we give a share of land to each person on our family gift list. This Christmas we are giving a community gift of a forty-acre tract of land in Blackfoot, Idaho, which we bought by mail for $720 through a sealed bid to the United States Government. Each person will receive a "certificate" for two-and-a-half acres.

We have followed this procedure now for three years, and our surprise is a delight to all. We spend only a little more than before and we save on wrapping and mailing.

Let the children buy their own washing machines, we say. We want to give a glamour gift they will all remember.

Should this way of giving ever work a hardship on us, we will give it up, because we know that our greatest kindness to the children is self-protection for us. But as long as we can give them shares in a community gift that will appreciate in value, this is what we will do. We're heroes on December 25, and the shopping is really an adventure.

35

THREE HAPPINESS GUARANTEES THAT INSURE PLEASURE ANYWHERE

You may be living lavishly, now that the children are gone, in three or four beautifully furnished and well-staffed homes or you may be living simply in a quiet cottage. Either way you can be happy or unhappy depending on your approach to life. This attitude has little to do with your bank account, but it is dependent on three happiness-makers which are available to every empty nester.

Three basic happiness-makers

When you are at home or traveling, alone or with others, spending lots or little, your life will be happy if you approach it with *enthusiasm, ease, and elegance.* At home or traveling follow these three simple rules: (1) Be enthusiastic about wherever you find yourself—or make a change. (2) Take an easy approach to life at home or abroad. (3) Live with elegance always.

THE SECRET OF UNFORCED ENTHUSIASM

In an environment that is physically and psychologically comfortable, enthusiasm comes naturally; in an unpleasant one, it is hard to work up. So get yourself comfortable, and keep your mind and your eyes wide open as you see what you can see. Enthusiasm for life is bound to come, and with enthusiasm come fun and friends.

DO THINGS THE EASY WAY

No matter how lavish, your surroundings will not be appreciated if you have to work day and night to keep things up. So in selecting any home or travel experience, ask yourself this question: Is this life going to be easy for me? If not, find an easier place or way.

ELEGANT LIVING EVERYWHERE

Remember, elegance in everyday living depends on attention to detail, taste, and maintenance. Understand this, and the size of your bank account will be inconsequential; in fact, traveling light will make everyday elegance easier to come by. Look for elegance wherever you stay and in whatever you buy, and life will take on luster.

No final retirement plan ever

Naturally, you are enthusiastic about the elegant new home you are moving into today, but know at the same time that ten years from now you may move to another that will bring just as much pleasure then. So never say, "This is it forever." Say, "This is it for now." Who knows? New circumstances may present an opportunity later on for an even more stimulating environment.

Flexibility is the sign of a big mind and the opportunity for new experiences is one of the delights of empty nest living. So welcome change when it suggests itself, for the adventure it can bring. And make no final "this is where we stay" plan, ever. *Living with zest implies motion.* Stay free and you will be young at heart forever. Stay young at heart, and life in your empty nest can be the happiest time of all.

BIBLIOGRAPHY

Gallup, George, *The Miracle Ahead,* Harper & Row, New York, 1964.

Hauser, Gayelord, *Mirror, Mirror on the Wall, Invitation to Beauty,* Farrar, Straus & Giroux, New York, 1961.

Hunt, Morton M., *Her Infinite Variety—The American Woman as Lover, Mate and Rival,* Harper & Row, New York, 1962.

Kent, Patricia, *An American Woman and Alcohol,* Holt, Rinehart and Winston, New York, 1967.

Kinney, Jean and Cle, *How to Get 20 to 90% Off on Everything You Buy,* Parker Publishing, West Nyack, New York, 1966.

Mann, Marty, *New Primer on Alcoholism,* Holt, Rinehart and Winston, New York, 1958.

Masters, Dr. William H. and Virginia Johnson, *Human Sexual Response,* Little, Brown, Boston, 1966.

Montagu, Ashley, *The Natural Superiority of Women,* The Macmillan Company, New York, 1953. Rev. ed., 1968.

Page, Dr. Robert Collier, *How to Lick Executive Stress,* Prentice-Hall, Englewood Cliffs, New Jersey, 1969.

Report of the President's Commission on the Status of Women and Other Publications of the Commission *American Women,* Scribner, New York, 1965.

INDEX

G

Gallup, Dr. George, 23
Gardening, 74, 142, 181, 219–220
General Education and Training program (GEDT), 143
Goddard College, 144–145
"Going Dutch," 181n.
Goldwater, Monroe, 213
Government employees, retirement plans of, 80–82
Grandchildren, 186–190
Grooming and makeup, courses in, 141

H

Halsman, Philippe, 138n., 194
Hammond, E. Cuyler, 15
Harris poll, 217
Hauser, Gayelord, 9, 233
Hays, Kathryne, 140
Head Start, 31n., 126n., 127–128
Headache, 6, 26, 39
Heart disease, 12–15
Heritage Village, Connecticut, 74, 84
High school equivalency, 143
Home decoration, 140
See also Furniture
Home economics, 147–148
Hometown, and retirement plans, 73, 76
Hormones
female, 25, 26–27, 40n., 46
male, 22, 47–48
Hospitals, volunteer work for, 125, 126–127, 128, 137
Hotel management, 142
Housatonic Psychiatric Center, xiv, 51
Houses
refurnishing of, 92–94
remodeling of, 66–67, 73, 78–79, 86, 103, 109
sale of, 67, 69
Hudson, Dr. John W., 49
Human Sexual Response (Masters and Johnson), 47, 233

Hurricane Camille, 210
Husic, John J., 149–150
Hypertension, 6, 26

I

Idaho
land purchased in, 227
vacation trips in, 208
Illinois, vacation trips in, 209
Income-tax return, 66n., 67, 103n., 104
Indianapolis, anticrime crusade in, 129
Industry, part-time work in, 156
Inheritance, 99, 113, 225, 226–227
Institute of Temporary Services, 149
Insurance, 105, 106, 224, 226
International Executive Business Corps, 133
International Training Systems, Inc., 142
Investments, 103, 105, 107, 108–113, 140, 163, 223, 224
Iowa, one-day drives in, 201–202
Iron Mountain Farm, 199, 200
Ironing, as profession, 158
Irving, Annabel, 199–201

J

Job applications, 154–155
Johnson, Virginia, 47, 233

K

Kannel, Dr. William B., 14n.
Kearney, Kevin E., 146
Kellogg Foundation, 148
Keppler, Victor, 193
Keys, Dr. Ancel, 12
Kinney, Cle, 93–96, 130, 197, 203, 233
Kircheimer, Mrs. Joseph, 125